HAVE FAITH IN YOUR KITCHEN

The Faith Fairchild Mysteries
by Katherine Hall Page

The Body in the Belfry
The Body in the Kelp
The Body in the Bouillon
The Body in the Vestibule
The Body in the Cast
The Body in the Basement
The Body in the Bog
The Body in the Fjord
The Body in the Bookcase
The Body in the Big Apple
The Body in the Moonlight
The Body in the Bonfire
The Body in the Lighthouse
The Body in the Attic
The Body in the Snowdrift
The Body in the Ivy
The Body in the Gallery
The Body in the Sleigh

Have Faith in Your Kitchen

Katherine Hall Page

Orchises • Washington

2010

Copyright © 2010 Katherine Hall Page

Library of Congress Cataloging-in-Publication Data
Page, Katherine Hall.
  Have faith in your kitchen / Katherine Hall Page.
     p. cm.
  Includes bibliographical references.
  ISBN 978-1-932535-23-5 (limited hardcover edition : alk. paper)
  — ISBN 978-1-932535-22-8 (pbk. edition : alk. paper)
  1. Cookery. 2. Fairchild, Faith Sibley (Fictitious character) I. Title.
  TX714.P134 2010
  641.5—dc22
                                                    2010007052

ACKNOWLEDGEMENTS

Material from *The Body in the Cast* by Katherine Hall Page © 1993 by the author and reprinted by permission of Minotaur Books, an imprint of St. Martin's Press, LLC, and from *The Body in the Basement* by Katherine Hall Page © 1994 by the author and reprinted by permission of Minotaur Books, an imprint of St. Martin's Press, LLC.

Material from *The Body in the Bog, The Body in the Fjord, The Body in the Bookcase, The Body in the Big Apple, The Body in the Moonlight, The Body in the Bonfire, The Body in the Lighthouse, The Body in the Attic, The Body in the Snowdrift, The Body in the Ivy, The Body in the Gallery,* and *The Body in the Sleigh* © 1996-2009 by Katherine Hall Page. Courtesy of HarperCollins Publishers.

COVER: JEAN FOGELBERG

Orchises Press
P. O. Box 320533
Alexandria, VA 22320-4533

G 6 E 4 C 2 A

TO MY READERS, OLD AND NEW

Le mauvais gout mène au crime.

Bad taste leads to crime.

—Baron Adolphe de Mareste (1784-1867)

Table of Contents

INTRODUCTION *i*

APPETIZERS / SMALL PLATES
Endive Spears with Chèvre *15*
Pear Brie Pizzette *16*
Alsacienne Onion Tarte *18*
Chicken Liver/Mushroom Pâté *20*
Chèvre / Red Onion / Roasted Pepper Sandwich *21*
Smørbrød Open Faced Sandwiches *22*
Faith's Emergency Sewing Circle Spreads: Chutney Cheese and Chèvre with Herbs *24*

AUTHOR'S NOTES
The Body in the Cast 25
The Body in the Moonlight 25
The Body in the Basement 28

SOUPS
Butternut Squash Soup *29*
Unadulterated Black Bean *30*
Apology Mushroom Soup *31*
Pasta e Fagioli with Sausage *33*
Avocado Bisque *34*
Pix Rowe Miller's Family Fish Chowder *35*
Fennel Soup *37*
Pumpkin Pie Soup *38*
Pantry / Fridge Soup *39*

AUTHOR'S NOTES
The Body in the Bookcase 41
The Body in the Fjord 42
The Body in the Bog 44

MAIN DISHES
VEGETARIAN
Spanakòpeta Greek Spinach Pie *46*
Cousin Luise's Linguini with Asparagus *47*
Pasta Frittata *48*

CHICKEN, BEEF, AND PORK
Chicken Stroganoff *49*
Boeuf Bourguinon (Beef Stew) *52*
Smothered Pork Chops *54*
Norwegian Meatballs *55*
Coq Au Vin *56*
Pork Loin Stuffed with Winter Fruits *57*
Faith's Yankee Pot Roast *58*
Pasta With Smoked Chicken Summer Vegetables *59*

SEAFOOD
Asian Noodles With Crabmeat *60*
Seafood Risotto *61*
Fiskepudding with Shrimp Sauce *62*
Lutefisk *65*
Crab Cakes *67*

AUTHOR'S NOTES
The Body in the Big Apple 68
The Body in the Bonfire 70
The Body in the Lighthouse 72

VEGETABLES, SIDE DISHES AND SALADS
Polenta with Gorgonzola *75*
Parsnip Puree *76*
Llapingachos with Salsa de Mali Potato Cakes with Peanut Sauce *77*
Corn Pudding *79*
Salad with Warm Cheese Toasts *80*
Aleford Baked Beans *81*
Waldorf Salad *83*
Cucumber and Dill Salad *84*
Mini Zucchini Fritters *85*

AUTHOR'S NOTES
The Body in the Attic 86
The Body in the Snowdrift 88

NOT-JUST-FOR-BREAKFAST DISHES
Blueberry Muffins *91*
Doughnut Muffins *92*
Southern Corn Bread *93*
Big Apple Pancakes *94*
Cardamom Raisin Bread *95*
"The Annie" Breakfast Sandwich *96*
Patriot's Day Pancakes *97*
Vafler—Sour Cream Waffles *98*

AUTHOR'S NOTES
The Body in the Ivy 99
The Body in the Snowdrift 101

JUST DESSERTS
Cambridge Tea Cake *105*
Glad's Brownies *106*
Red Velvet Cake *107*
Aunt Susie's Cake *109*
Chocolate Bread Pudding *110*
Harvard Squares *112*
Comfort Cookies *113*
Betty's Oatmeal Lace Cookies *114*
Rhubarb Crumble *115*
Norwegian Christmas Cake—Mør Monsen's Kake *116*
French Apple Cake *118*
Manhattan Morsels *119*
Bainbridge Butterscotch Shortbread *120*
Oatmeal Chocolate Goodies *121*
Faith Fairchild's Maine Blueberry Tarte *122*
Pelham Fudge Cake *124*
Lizzie's Sour Cream Brownies *125*
Pepperkaker (Ginger Snaps) *126*
Mrs. Mallory's Peanut Butter Cookies *127*
Lizzie's Flourless Peanut Butter Cookies *128*
Lizzie's Sugar and Spice Cookies *129*
Denouement Apple / Pear Crisp *130*
(Virtually) Flourless Chocolates Cakes *131*
Chocolate Crunch Cookies *132*

AUTHOR'S NOTES
The Body in the Sleigh 133

APPENDIX
(Recipes by Book) *139*

INTRODUCTION

Faith Sibley Fairchild, the amateur sleuth in my mystery series, is among other things a caterer. When I started writing the first book, *The Body in the Belfry* (1990), my husband was on sabbatical and we were living in Lyon, France. Each day, I'd shop in an open air market that stretched for blocks along the Quai St. Antoine, and watch as Paul Bocuse selected his ingredients for that evening's three star meals before following in his footsteps to select the ingredients for my more humble attempts. Back at the apartment, after putting the food away, I wrote. I liked mysteries with food in them—Rex Stout, Dorothy Sayers, Nan and Ivan, Virginia Rich—but I think Faith Fairchild was a product not just of my imagination, but the sights and smells of all that fabulous food in Lyon. (The wonderfully fresh baguettes never made it up my long flights of stairs intact-the heel was always missing by the time I opened my door).

Have Faith in Your Kitchen has been a work in progress since I first started putting recipes at the end of the books, starting with *The Body in the Cast* (1993). All the recipes are original, either created by me or the individual credited. The dishes are straightforward—anyone can make them—and require no expensive or exotic ingredients. In some cases, I've also suggested ways they can be modified to make them more heart-wise. The appendix lists the recipes by each book; some play a more prominent role in the plots than others.

The Faith Fairchild mysteries fall into the traditional mystery category. They are puzzle mysteries and readers will find more humor than dismembered body parts—much more, in fact. There are no dismembered parts. At the start of the series, Faith is living in Aleford, a small, fictitious suburb West of Boston where she has moved following her marriage to the Reverend Thomas Fairchild. Daughter and granddaughter of clergy, Faith had sworn to avoid the fishbowl existence parish life inevitably offers, plus she had no intention of ever leaving Manhattan where she was born and raised. But the heart knows no reason and by the time she realizes the handsome man she's been flirting with over the coulibiac of salmon at a wedding she's catering is the same person who just performed the ceremony, it's too late. Soon she's entrenched in the more bucolic orchards of New England complaining about boiled dinners and missing everything about the Big Apple. Stumbling across the still warm corpse of a parishioner in the town's old belfry sends her off in the lively pursuit of miscreants over eighteen books (and counting). In the first book, she has baby Benjamin; he acquires a sister, Amy in the fourth. The Aleford books alternate with other locales—Maine, Vermont, Norway, France, and yes, New York City.

Beginning with the fourth book, I started adding an Author's Note at the end where I stepped from behind the curtain and wrote about subjects ranging from funeral baked meats to reading cookbooks purely for pleasure. These have been scattered throughout *Have Faith in Your Kitchen* as kinds of condiments to accompany the recipes.

Thanks are due to many people, first and foremost, my friend Roger Lathbury and Orchises Press. It has been such a joy to do this book with him. Also my agent, Faith Hamlin, who has been with me since the beginning. And special thanks to the following who helped with recipes: Kyra Alex, Helen Barer, Carol Bischoff, Elizabeth Bledsoe, Gladys Boalt, the late Ethel Clifford , Hege Farstad, David Fine, Susan Houston, Luise Kleinberg, David Pologe, and Elizabeth Samenfeld-Specht,.

Finally, to my two beloved tasters, Alan and Nicholas.

Have Faith in Your Kitchen

Appetizers / Small Plates

Endive Spears with Chèvre

2 heads endive
Fig vinegar (Cuisine Perel brand if possible)
5 ounces fresh chèvre at room temperature
4 ounces cream cheese at room temperature
1 tablespoon half-and-half or light cream
Whole shelled walnuts

Look for endive that is fresh and a tight head. If you can, find the slightly purple variety, it's nice to alternate the spears on your serving platter.

Discard the outer leaf and cut a thin slice from the bottom to make it easier to remove the leaves. You may have to do this again. Save the small core of inner leaves for a future salad.

Lightly brush the spears with the vinegar.

Arrange the spears in a circular rows or any other way that is attractive on a serving platter or tray.

Combine the two cheeses and half-and-half in a food processor and pulse until creamed together. Fill a pastry bag with the mixture and pipe about a tablespoon on the wide end of the spear. You may also spoon the mixture on the spear. Top with a walnut half. In season you can use pomegranate seeds or a piece of fresh fig. Dried cranberry is also good or a piece of candied ginger for a very different taste.

You can prepare the cheese mixture ahead of time and refrigerate, bringing it to room temperature before assembling. Serves 6.

Pear Brie Pizzette

Dough:

1 cup warm water
1 package granular yeast (not rapid-rising)
1 teaspoon sugar
1 1/2 teaspoons salt
1 tablespoon olive oil
2 1/2-3 cups all-purpose flour
Cornmeal

Pour the water in a bowl and sprinkle the yeast on top. Add the sugar, salt, olive oil, and mix until the yeast is dissolved. Add 1 1/2 cups of flour, stir, and add 1 more cup. Combine thoroughly and turn the dough out onto a lightly floured surface, adding the rest of the flour if the dough is too sticky. Knead for 5 minutes.

Put the dough in a lightly oiled bowl and let rise in a warm place until double in bulk—about 1 hour. Punch down and divide into 2 pieces for the pizzettes. Let the dough rest for about 15 minutes. Using a rolling pin or your hands, shape into 2 flat rounds.

Topping:

3 large yellow onions
1 tablespoon olive oil
1 tablespoon unsalted butter
1 1/2 tablespoons sugar
2 large ripe pears (Comice are especially good)
1/2-3/4 pound ripe, but not runny, Brie

Preheat the oven to 450°.

Slice the onions into thing rings and sauté in the melted butter and oil until limp. Cover the pan, stirring occasionally. Cook slowly for about 15 minutes. Uncover the pan, sprinkle the onions with the sugar, turn up the heat and cook until well browned. Stir constantly. The sugar caramelizes the onions. This will take 15-20 minutes. Set the onions aside.

Peel and slice the pears.

Brush the tops of the pizzettes with some olive oil and spread the caramelized onions over each. Arrange the pear slices on top and dot with slices of the Brie.

Bake for 15 minutes on a lightly greased pizza pan on which you've sprinkled cornmeal. The dough may also be shaped into a large rectangle and baked on a cookie sheet and cut into squares. Serves 4—more if served as a first course.

Alsacienne Onion Tarte

Pastry:
1 1/2 cups flour
Pinch of salt
12 tablespoons unsalted butter, cut into pieces
3 tablespoons ice water

Place the flour, salt, and butter in the bowl of a food processor and add the ice water through the tube with the machine running. Stop as soon as the dough forms a ball. Wrap it in Saran and refrigerate for 30 minutes.

You may also make the pastry by hand, cutting the butter into the flour and salt, then adding the water and shaping the dough into a ball before refrigerating.

You may also use prepared piecrust.

After refrigerating, roll the pastry out and line a 9-inch pie tin or quiche pan. Refrigerate again while you are making the filling.

Filling:
2 slices bacon, cut into pieces
1 1/2 cups, approx. 2 medium, yellow onions thinly sliced
2 tablespoons flour
2 cups milk
1/2 cup light cream
3 large eggs
1/4 teaspoon freshly ground pepper
1/8 teaspoon freshly ground nutmeg

Fry the bacon until it is crisp. Add the onions and sauté for 3-4 minutes. Sprinkle the flour over the mixture and stir. Add the milk and bring the mixture to a boil, stirring constantly.

Turn the heat down and simmer for 3-4 minutes.

Remove the pan from the heat and let it cool for 10 minutes. Beat the eggs and cream together and add them, the pepper and nutmeg to the onion/bacon/milk mixture.

Pour the filling into the pastry shell. Place it on a cookie sheet. Cook the tarte in the middle of a preheated 400° oven for approximately 45 minutes. Check after 40 minutes. The crust should be lightly browned and the filling firm. Serves 8.

Faith caramelized the onions for her luncheon, but it isn't necessary for the dish. Try it as a variation if you prefer. You may also add some freshly chopped parsley or other herbs to the filling after you have sautéed the onions. Whole milk makes for a creamier tarte, but 1% or 2% tastes fine also.

Chicken Liver/Mushroom Pâté

1/2 pound chicken livers
1/2 cup unsalted butter
1 medium yellow onion, chopped
1 clove garlic, minced
4 ounces mushroom, chopped
1 tablespoon Port
1/8 teaspoon ground nutmeg
Salt
Freshly ground pepper
Clarified butter, optional

After cutting any gristle from the livers, heat six tablespoons of butter in a pan large enough for all the livers and cook them quickly, approximately three minutes on a side. Remove the livers with a slotted spoon and place in the bowl of a food processor or a blender container.

Add the onion and garlic to the pan and cook until soft. Add the mushrooms and cook the mixture for five minutes, stirring occasionally. Add to the livers.

Melt the rest of the butter in the pan and stir in the Port. Add to the liver mixture. Process until smooth. Add the nutmeg, then salt and pepper to taste. Transfer the pâté into a small crock.

Cover it with a thin layer of clarified butter if you wish to keep it for more than two days. Refrigerate when cool. Makes about 1 1/4 cups.

This recipe doubles well and should be made a day ahead. It is a wonderfully rich, versatile pâté and works as well on thin toast for a dinner party or slathered on baguettes for a picnic.

Chèvre / Red Onion / Roasted Pepper Sandwich

Fresh Chèvre—goat's milk cheese
Thinly sliced red onion
Roasted red and yellow peppers
Extra-virgin olive oil
Bread: sourdough, country or peasant bread, foccacia

To assemble the sandwich, first drizzle a small amount of oil on both slices of the bread, unless you are using foccacia, which already has plenty of oil. Then spread a generous amount of the chèvre on the bread, and add a layer of peppers. Separate the onions into thin rings, add them on top of the peppers and top with the remaining slice of bread. Press down gently, wrap in saran wrap, and keep cool unless you are eating it immediately. An herbed fresh chèvre is also delicious in this sandwich.

Note on roasting peppers: For years, Faith roasted peppers either on a grill or by placing cored and seeded peppers, cut in half, skin side up, under the broiler until the skin charred. Then she put them in a plastic bag, shut it tightly and after about fifteen minutes, took the peppers out and peeled them. Now she roasts, rather than broils them in the oven by first preheating to 350° F, then seeding and quartering the peppers before tossing them with 1/8 cup of olive oil and Kosher or sea salt to taste for every four large peppers. The peppers are placed in a single layer in a baking dish and covered with aluminum foil before they are placed in the oven for about an hour to an hour and a half. They need to be turned occasionally, so they don't scorch. When they are removed from the oven, Faith often adds a dash of balsamic vinegar and does not peel them. Having a container of these in the refrigerator means you have one of the ingredients for this sandwich, but also the start of an antipasto platter or a sauce for pasta.

Smørbrød

Open Faced Sandwiches

If you have traveled in Scandinavia, you have some idea how delicious—and addictive —these are. The point is to compose something as appealing to the eye as the palate and a buffet of several different kinds of smørbrød makes for a good party, aquavit or no aquavit.

The bread, which may be white, wheat, rye, whole grain, whatever you like, acts as the platform for the creation. Slice the bread thin, but thick enough to hold what you will be arranging on top. Spread it with unsalted butter or herb butter. After the butter, most sandwiches start with a lettuce leaf, but you can also use other thinly sliced vegetables. Smørbrød are eaten with a knife and fork. Thick bread detracts from the taste of the other ingredients and is also hard to cut through.

Generally, white bread is used for more delicate flavors, like shrimp. Heartier breads for things like smoked fish or roast beef.

To make Pix's favorite, spread the bread lightly with unsalted butter, add a leaf of Boston lettuce, then arrange several rows of small cooked shrimp on top. Pipe some mayonnaise (Norwegian mayonnaise is a bit sweeter than Hellmann's) from a pastry tube on top of the shrimp. Cut a thin slice of lemon, remove the seeds, cut it almost crosswise and twist it, placing it across the shrimp.

Other good combinations are:

Roast beef topped with a thin slice of tomato and horseradish mayonnaise

Thin grilled room temperature meat patty (beef or veal) topped with fried onions

Smoked salmon topped by thin asparagus spears that have been marinated in vinaigrette and a final dollop of crème fraîche

Smoked salmon topped with slices of cucumber dill salad

Slices of hard cooked egg topped with anchovies or herring and tomato slices

Smoked mussels or smoked eel on top of scrambled egg

Sliced liverwurst topped with crisp bacon and garnished with a sliced cornichon, the small, tart French gherkin

Jarlsberg cheese with turkey topped by a spoonful of chutney

And so forth!

It is important to put enough on the sandwich, so the bread is hidden.

It is also important to decorate the surface with chopped parsley, a carrot curl, sprigs of herbs, capers, caviar, strips of pimento or peppers fanned to make a floral shape, or lemon.

The sandwiches are served on large trays or platters that have been covered with paper doilies.

Faith's Emergency Sewing Circle Spreads: Chutney Cheese and Chèvre with Herbs

Chutney Cheese:

8 ounces plain cream cheese, room temperature
1 cup chutney

Cream the chutney and cheese together by hand. Do not use a food processor or blender otherwise you end up with cheese sauce. Pix uses her own green tomato chutney, which is a spicy combination of tomatoes, onions, raisins, and walnuts. All and any varieties of chutney work well.

Chèvre with Herbs:

4 ounces plain cream cheese, room temperature
4-5 ounces chèvre (100% goat's milk cheese)
Herbs to taste

Herbed chèvre, and other flavors, are readily available in most markets and cheese stores. To keep things simple, use one of these. Combine the cheeses by hand. The cream cheese makes the combination easier to spread. If you are using fresh herbs, rosemary, tarragon, and summer savory are good choices alone or in combination.

Use both spreads to stuff snow or sugar snap peas, spread on cucumber or zucchini rounds, sweetmeal biscuits, water biscuits, or slightly toasted miniature bagels. The chutney spread makes a tasty sandwich when combined with smoked turkey, Virginia ham, or by itself on date and nut or buckwheat walnut breads.

The Body in the Cast

I apologize to all of you who have been asking for recipes. I should have done them sooner, but when I wrote my first book, *The Body in the Belfry*, I thought it might seem I was borrowing more than a cup of sugar from the late Virginia Rich, one of my favorite mystery writers, who included recipes in her books. I was also afraid recipes might distract readers from the plot. You would be so busy deciding whether to put Spanish or Vidalia onions in your soup that you'd miss a red herring. However, here they are at last. I hope they will give you as much pleasure as they do my family.

Faith is a purist. I am not. People in fiction seem to have a great deal more time than the people I know in real life, with nine to five jobs, gardens to weed, and wash to do (plus that stack of books next to the bed). These recipes will all taste fine with modifications such as good canned beef stock, instead of homemade, for the meatballs (although not canned bread crumbs) and already-prepared pizza dough, like Boboli, for the pizzette. You can also made the cookies ahead and freeze the balls, baking a batch when you need—or want—them. The point is to end up with something tasty to sit down to with the latest Faith Fairchild mystery propped up next to your plate. *Santé!*

The Body in the Moonlight

Faith's bedside table—and mine—are piled high with mysteries, of course, but also with cookbooks. In Faith's case, cooking is a vocation, as well as avocation, so she is reading for business and pleasure. I've always enjoyed reading cookbooks the way I read novels, picturing the meals, creating settings in much the same manner that characters and plots come to life in my imagination as I turn those pages. It is important to approach the reading of cookbooks with the firm resolve that actually cooking anything from them is not necessary, otherwise guilt creeps in like a boring dinner guest and you're reaching for pad and pencil instead of simply having fun.

There are a number of mystery cookbooks that pleasantly combine the genres. Three of my favorites are: *The Nero Wolfe Cookbook*, Rex Stout and the Editors of Viking Press, 1973; *The Lord Peter Wimsey Cookboo*k, Elizabeth Bond Ryan and William J. Eakins, 1981; and *Madame Maigret's Recipes*, Robert J. Courtine (collected in honor of Georges Simenon's seventieth birthday), 1975.

In his novel, *A Duet, with an Occasional Chorus*, Arthur Conan Doyle refers to Mrs. Beeton as "the finest housekeeper in the world." and notes that her book "has more wisdom to the square inch than any work of man." *Household Management* contained over 80,000 square inches of information, so this was high praise indeed. Mrs. Beeton is a fine place to start for recreational cookery reading. Besides recipes, Mrs. Beeton provides "instructions for servants who wait at table," lovely diagrams for napkin folding, specific instructions for laying a table—twenty-four inches for "each person's accommodation"—and not only supplies a chart for the housewife's work week, starting with Monday-washing, but instructs her on how to select said house or flat, furnish it, and obtain letters of introduction to the neighbors.

In this country, we had Fannie Farmer. My oldest copy is from 1915, and like Mrs. Beeton, contains illustrations that are a window into a time when women, Martha Stewart notwithstanding, had the time to garnish and frill. Besides such interesting items as "Broiled Oranges on Toast" and "Sweetbreads à la Root" (truffles, carrots, onions, celery, pureéd chestnuts, mushrooms and somewhere in all that, the sweetbreads), the author provides a surprisingly tasty sounding recipe for "Chicken à la King", that staple of my high school cafeteria. I think they must have left out the butter and cream, but I do remember those canned pimientos.

Library book sales, yard and rummage sales are treasure troves for old cookbooks and aside from their historical interest—the way we ate—they also offer more intimate connections with the past. Inscriptions to brides, mothers, daughters, and new homeowners give us a sense of connection, especially if the recipients have annotated the book. I recently picked up a gem, Marian Tracy's *New Casserole Cookery*. The original *Casserole Cookery* went on sale the day after Pearl Harbor, I learned recently. It was still my mother's mainstay in the late forties and early fifties. We would never have dared to criticize her nightly offerings, but the words, "dish of infamy", accurately describe some of the attempts. The previous owner of my *New Casserole Cookery* was a scribbler, and a pithy one. Next to "Roquefort Meat Loaf", she (her name is in the front) wrote, and underlined, "Lousy." "Turkey and Apple Casserole" was "nasty"; "Turkey and Cranberry Roll," "awful"—to describe a few. "Baked Peppers with Macaroni and Sausage" rated a "very good" with a note to be sure to "really parboil the peppers—it's all the cooking they get." For whom was she writing these notes—reminders to herself? For posterity? I wish I could meet her. Old cookbooks often have recipes clipped from magazines or recipes on index cards tucked in the pages like messages in a bottle.

Cookbooks that combine reminiscence or personal reflections with recipes are especially appealing—especially poignant when the author is gone—Craig Claiborne's *A Feast Made for Laughter*, Laurie Colwin's *Home Cooking* and *More Home Cooking*, everything M.F.K. Fisher wrote.

The favorites march on: all of Elizabeth David, Sara Kasdan's *Mazel Tov Y'All*, Calvin Trillin's Tummy Trilogy—*American Fried*, *Alice, Let's Eat*, and *Third Helpings*, Sylvia Woods' *Sylvia's Family Soul Food Cookbook*, Mimi Sheraton's *From My Mother's Kitchen*, Peg Bracken's "I Hate to Cook" books, Jane Grigson's *Food With the Famous*.

After reading my last book, *The Body in the Big Apple*, a friend called, not to talk about the mystery, but to ask if by chance I had the recipe for the Horn and Hardart Automat's macaroni and cheese I so lovingly described. Reading about it had instantly taken her back to her childhood and the excitement of putting the nickels in the slot, then lifting up the little glass door to remove for the small dark green casserole filled with the fragrant dish. I didn't have the recipe, but tracked it down in Molly O'Neill's *New York Cookbook*. Nach Waxman, of Kitchen Arts and Letters in Manhattan, who helped me find it said people ask for Automat recipes all the time. Food is a powerful mnemonic in our lives and reading about it surrounds us with both comfort and desire. When you add mystery as an ingredient, the result takes the cake.

The Body in the Basement

There are cooks—and cooks. Pix represents one school; Faith another. I fall somewhere in between. As with the recipes in *The Body in the Cast*, these can be made successfully by cooks of all natures. Substitutions have been suggested in some cases and certainly feel free to experiment. I'm told I make a great chili, but since I put different things in each time depending on what's to hand, I may never develop a recipe for it.

A relative once told me that anyone who could read could cook, a notion I heartily endorse. Cookbooks are always in the stack of books next to my bed (along with mysteries). Crime and food go together well. Occasionally a passion for one will lead to the other—as in Faith's and my cases. There's nothing we enjoy more than sitting in the backyard with a plate of Bainbridge Shortbread and a cup of tea…or a glass of wine and a stack of crackers and Chutney Cheese or…being transported to whatever world a favorite mystery author has chosen this time. I hope you will join us.

Soups

Butternut Squash Soup

1 medium-sized (approximately 3 lb.) butternut squash
1 medium-sized yellow onion
2 cups chicken stock
Water, if necessary
1/2 cup Half and Half
3/4 teaspoon freshly grated nutmeg
Salt and pepper to taste

Peel and seed the squash. This is easier to do if you cut it into several pieces first. Cut the prepared squash into chunks and place them in a stockpot or similar large pot. Peel the onion and cut it into four pieces. Add these to the pot. Pour in the stock, unsalted if you are using canned stock. If the stock does not cover the vegetables, add water. Cover, bring to a boil, then turn the heat down to medium low and simmer until you can pierce the squash with a fork. Purée in batches in a blender or food processor and return to the pot. Add the Half and Half, nutmeg, salt, and pepper. Serve with a dollop of crème fraîche and grate a hint of nutmeg on top. Serves 8 as a first course or 6 as a main course.

This soup may be made the day before and refrigerated. It is also a base for other squash soups. For Curried Squash Soup, add a peeled and seeded apple cut into quarters with the onion and replace the nutmeg with curry powder. For Squash and Roasted Red Pepper Soup, add two roasted red peppers with the onion and replace the nutmeg with 1/8 teaspoon of red pepper flakes.

A heart-wise recipe, this soup also tastes delicious without the Half and Half and no salt at all.

Unadulterated Black Bean Soup

1 pound dried black beans
2 ham hocks or 1 ham bone
2 medium onions, 1 red and 1 yellow
7-8 cups water
1/2 teaspoon salt
1/4 teaspoon freshly ground pepper
1 tablespoon dry sherry or Madeira (optional)
Sour cream
Chives

Pick over the beans, rinse, cover with cold water and bring to a boil for 2 minutes. Remove from heat and let stand for at least 1 hour. (Or soak the beans overnight.)

Rinse the ham hocks. Peel and quarter the onions. Bury the hocks and onions in the beans. Add 7-8 cups cold water and bring to a boil. Turn the heat down and simmer 1 1/2 to 2 hours.
Be sure the beans are soft.

Remove the hocks or bone and strip any meat from the. Add the meat to the soup and puree the mixture in batches in a blender. (Note: a food processor sometimes leaks with this much liquid.) Put the pureed soup in a clean pot; warm, adding the seasonings and wine if used.

Serve with a dollop of sour cream and finely mined chives. For a special party, put the sour cream in a pastry tube and pipe 2 concentric circles on top of each serving of soup. Take a sharp knife and pull it through the circles, first toward the center, then away, for a nice spider web effect.

This soup tastes better if made a day ahead. Serves 8 to 10, more as a first course.

Apology Mushroom Soup

1/2 cup Madeira
1 ounce dried morels or other dried mushrooms
2 3/4 cups unsalted chicken broth
3 leeks, the white parts
1 medium yellow onion
4 tablespoons butter
3 tablespoons flour
2 3/4 cups unsalted beef broth
1 pound fresh mushrooms, stems removed and sliced
1 teaspoon salt
1/2 teaspoon pepper
Sour cream or crème fraîche (optional)

Combine the Madeira, 1/2 cup of the chicken broth, and the dried mushrooms in a small saucepan. Cover and bring to a boil, then set aside off the heat for 30 minutes.

While the mushrooms are soaking, clean and slice the leeks. Dice the onion. Melt the butter is a large soup pot and sauté the leeks and onions until they are soft, about 10 minutes. Sprinkle the mixture with the flour and continue to cook for 5 more minutes.

Add the remaining chicken broth, the beef broth, the fresh mushrooms, the dried mushrooms and their soaking liquid, the salt, and pepper. Simmer covered for 10 minutes, then uncovered for 20 minutes more.

Cool the soup slightly and puree in batches in a blender or in the pot with an immersion blender. Return the soup to the pot and heat it through over low heat.

Serve with a generous dollop of sour cream or crème fraîche.

This makes a hearty supper dish and will serve 6. As a first course or luncheon dish, it will serve 8. Making the soup a day ahead improves the flavor.

I am indebted to my nephew, David Pologe, for this recipe and to his mother, Sheila, who first served it to me.

Pasta e Fagioli with Sausage

1 tablespoon olive oil
1 medium yellow onion, diced
2 medium carrots, diced
1 rib of celery, diced
1 large garlic clove, peeled and diced
2 cups canned, diced tomatoes with the juice
4 cups chicken broth, canned or home made
1/2 pound chourico or other cooked sausage sliced into 1/2" rounds
1 cup cooked and rinsed (if canned) cannellini or other white beans
1/2 cup ditalini or other short, tubular pasta
Salt and freshly ground pepper
2 tablespoons fresh basil leaves, minced
2 tablespoons fresh parsley leaves, minced
2 tablespoons grated Parmesan, Romano, or combination of both cheeses

Heat the olive oil in a heavy saucepan or stockpot and add the onions, carrots, celery and garlic. Stir and cook over medium heat until the onions are soft, approximately 2-3 minutes. Add the tomatoes and broth (if you can find these without salt or MSG, it's preferable). Bring the mixture to a boil. Add the sausage rounds. Reduce the heat, cover, and simmer for 20 minutes. Add the beans and pasta and cook, stirring often until the pasta is done, approximately 10 minutes. Season to taste with salt and pepper, remembering that the sausage may be salty. Add the basil and parsley. Serve with a sprinkling of cheese. Serves 6.
You can prepare this ahead of time, stopping before the beans and pasta, adding those and the rest of the ingredients shortly before serving.

Avocado Bisque

1 ripe avocado
2 cups chicken broth
1/2 cup heavy cream
1/2 cup light cream
2 tablespoons white rum (Preferably Mount Gay)
1/2 teaspoon curry powder
1/2 teaspoon salt
Freshly ground pepper

Peel the avocado and remove the pit. Cut the pulp in several pieces and place in a blender container with the chicken broth (cold), creams, rum, curry powder, salt, and a pinch of pepper. Blend until smooth. May be made ahead and kept refrigerated. Serves four. This recipe may be doubled.

The soup is a lovely color and Faith serves it in well chilled bouillon cups with a spider web garnish of slightly thinned sour cream, or thinned crème fraîche. Use a pastry tube to pipe two or three concentric circles on top of the soup, then take a sharp knife and pull it through the circles, first toward the center, then the next away from the center. A bright nasturtium in the middle adds a nice, elegant Martha Stewartish touch. Nasturtiums are edible. Avoid foxglove and the like.

Pix Rowe Miller's Family Fish Chowder

6-7 1/4" thick slices bacon
3 cups diced yellow onions
5-6 medium potatoes, peeled
1 lb. haddock
1 lb. cod
2 cans (3 cups) evaporated milk
1 cup whole milk
Salt
Freshly ground pepper

Fry the bacon, removed from the pan, and place on a paper towel. Sauté the onions in the bacon fat and set the pan aside.
Cut the potatoes in half the long way, then in 1/4" slices. Put them in a nonreactive pot large enough for the chowder. Cover the potatoes with water and boil until tender. Be careful not to put in too much water or the chowder will be soupy. While the potatoes are cooking, cut the fish into generous bite-sized pieces.

When the potatoes are ready, add the fish to the pot, cover and simmer until the fish flakes.

When the fish is done, crumble the bacon and add it to the pot along with the onions and any grease in the pan, the evaporated and whole milks. Bring the mixture to a boil, cover, and turn the heat down. Simmer for 5 minutes and add salt and pepper to taste.

Chowder invariably tastes better when made a day ahead.

The word "chowder" comes from the French, "la chaudière," a very large copper pot. Several centuries ago, French coastal villages would celebrate the safe return of their fishing fleets with a feast. The main course was a fish stew made in la chaudière into which each fisherman would toss part of his catch. "Chaudière" became "chowder" as the tradition made its way across the Atlantic to Canada and Down East. Chowders have continued to be just as idiosyncratic as these long ago concoctions. Pix does not even want to hear about the Manhattan version with tomato, but others are more open. The Rowe recipe may be happily modified in all sorts of ways.

This chowder is still quite delectable with olive oil instead of bacon fat. You may also use salt pork. Two kinds of fish make for a more interesting chowder, but these can be any combination of the following: haddock, cod, Pollack, monkfish, and hake. Finally, there is the question of garnishes: dill, chopped parsley, oyster crackers, butter are all good. And Faith and Pix's friend on Sanpere, Jane Weiss, swears by her chowder to which she adds curry spices!

Fennel Soup

1 large fennel bulb (about 1 pound)
1 large potato, peeled and diced (Yukon Golds are good)
4 cups chicken stock, preferably unsalted
1/2 medium yellow onion, peeled and diced
1/4 teaspoon tarragon
1/2 teaspoon salt
1/4 teaspoon freshly ground pepper
1/2 cup light cream or half-and-half
Seeds from half a pomegranate.

Cut the tall stalks from the fennel bulb, saving some of the feathery fronds for a garnish, if desired. Cut the bulb into chunks.

Put the fennel, potato, onion, and tarragon into a heavy saucepan. Add the chicken broth, bring the mixture to a boil, and simmer until the fennel and potato are soft.

Puree the mixture in a blender or food processor, return to the saucepan and add the cream or half-and-half. Salt and pepper to taste.

This soup tastes best warm, not piping hot. The pomegranate seeds add flavor and texture. This is a good cold summer soup, too. Try shrimp instead of the pomegranate seeds. Serves six.

Pumpkin Pie Soup

4 cups pumpkin puree (your own from a sugar pumpkin or canned)
4 cups chicken stock, preferably salt-free
3 tablespoons brown sugar
1 1/2 teaspoons cinnamon
1 teaspoon ground ginger
1 teaspoon nutmeg
1/2 teaspoon salt
2 cups half and half or light cream
Sour cream

Mix the first seven ingredients together in a large saucepan and bring to a simmer. Simmer for about 10 minutes. Turn the heat off and add the half and half. Let sit for 5 minutes and reheat gently. Serve with a dollop of sour cream to cut the sweetness.

Children love this nutritious dish. For all ages, it's fun to use a mug, piping a rosette of sour cream on top.

Pantry/Fridge Soup

2 tablespoons olive oil
1 large clove of garlic
1 onion
4-5 mushrooms
1 can tomatoes, diced or whole
1 can chickpeas or cannelini beans
4 cups chicken broth
4 chicken sausages, 12 ounce package
1/4 cup orzo or other small pasta such as ditalini or conchigliette
2 teaspoons dried rosemary
Salt and pepper to taste

Mince the garlic and dice the onion and mushrooms. You may use whatever onion you have in the fridge and any variety of mushrooms, adjusting the amount for size. For this dish, Faith used plain old white mushrooms and a yellow onion.

Heat the oil in a Dutch oven or other covered soup pot and sauté the garlic, onion, and mushrooms for about 5 minutes.

Rinse and add the chickpeas or beans. Add the tomatoes and seasonings. Almost any other herb may be used—thyme, oregano, parsley—and use fresh ones if handy. Add the broth, canned, in a box, or homemade. Bring the soup to a boil and add the sliced sausages.

Bring the soup back to the boil—it doesn't take long—and add the pasta. Cover and simmer until the pasta is done. Add grated cheese on top if you have some in your fridge or freezer. Serves 4.

The above is merely a template. Faith uses the chicken sausages, widely available now in a variety of flavors, because she always has some in her freezer and they make for a heartwise dish. You can substitute beef broth and beef or pork sausages. If you have scallions or shallots, use those instead of the onion. A pepper may be added to or replace the mushrooms. The beauty of this recipe is in its speed and how creative it makes the cook feel. Try the teriyaki ginger chicken sausages with garlic or sesame oil instead of olive oil. In season, add fresh chopped chard or kale a few minutes before serving. Leave out the pasta and serve with a warm crusty baguette or loaf of sour dough.

The Body in the Bookcase

The best of times; the worst of times—that's when we turn to food.

Whether it's a wake or sitting shiva, at some point, someone is bound to say, "Try to eat a little something." The Aleford casserole brigade springs into action after the Fairchilds are burglarized. We have all done the same thing, bearing lasagna pans, soup tureens, loaves of bread to the bereaved and distressed in body or mind. Offering food allows us to express our concern, our sorrow. We come bearing comfort food. Food that goes down easily—whatever that tradition may be. One person's chicken soup is another's spicy jambalaya.

Then we have celebratory food—wedding food. Memorable feasts. I've written about both kinds in this particular book and thoughts of all the funeral-baked meats, as well as festive nuptials kept me company. The mere mention of these foods is a mnemonic. I thought about the French country wedding we attended that started with rich brioche and champagne immediately following the ceremony, ending almost twenty-four hours, and many courses later, with onion soup gratineé. There was the wedding reception at the Boston Athaneum where the bride's mother and grandmother had made a fabulous, many tiered cake—decorated with words and edible objects that had special significance for the bride and groom. Our own wedding was at the home of the friends to whom this book is dedicated—deep in the woods, a miraculous December day filled with so much sunshine, guests sat outdoors to eat. A Nor'-easter dumped a foot of snow on the ground a week later. The food was delicious I'm told. Too nervous, excited to eat, both my husband and I were so ravenous late that night, we scoured the Connecticut countryside for an open sub shop on the way to our honeymoon inn. And what a sandwich it was—roasted peppers, steak, cheese. There was a fire in the room's fireplace and we ate, sipping champagne—a decidedly non-Faith Fairchild menu, but one we'll remember forever.

The sad times—those soups and casseroles, but also the platters of little sandwiches, the anchovy paste on cardboard. People, preoccupied with the business of grief, eat a triangle or two, then drift back together, gather about those stricken. I sometimes think these aluminum trays of sandwiches float from one living room, funeral home, church hall to another across the country, the crustless bread always white and slightly stale. Another tray holds slices of cake; there's always a coffee urn. We don't really remember the food, but know it was there. Remember the urgings, "You have to keep your strength up. Try some soup. Mrs.—fill in any name—made it."

Good times and bad times. We reach for and provide sustenance—the abundance of food, the offerings of our hearts common to both.

The Body in the Fjord

Just as the smell of coffee and cardamom reminded Ursula Rowe of the Hansen's kitchen, it transports me back to my grandparents' house. My grandfather, Peter Malmgreen, built it in his old age painting the shingles red, because my grandmother, Alfhild, was still homesick, even though they'd left Norway at the turn-of-the-century. She used to give us "coffee milk"—milk, sugar, and an inch or two of strong Maxwell House brew—the "Good to the Last Drop" factory was not far away in Hoboken and, more important, was a sponsor of the TV show "I Remember Mama."

My grandmother cooked the only food she knew—Norwegian, feeding a large family throughout the Depression. Some of these dishes became the favorites of my generation too, as our mothers prepared the kinds of meals they had grown up on—lured away on occasion by the "Casserole Cookery" craze of the fifties and forever changed by Craig Claiborne's hefty *New York Times Cookbook* (his Beef Stroganoff was de rigueur for an exotic dinner party all across the North Jersey suburbs in the early sixties.) Still, our comfort foods were my grandmother's—veal and beef meatballs with a hint of nutmeg, Tilslørtebondepiker with its toothsome layers of sweet toasted crumbs, applesauce, and whipped cream; fruit puddings (with more cream), and our frequent Sunday night supper—a bowl of bread, milk and sugar. At an early age, we also developed a fondness for herring—but drew the line at gjetost, a brown goat cheese, no matter how much my mother loved it.

Our koldtbord on Christmas Eve was to a child's eye, more splendid even than Kvikne's Hotel's—accompanied as it was by a multitude of cousins, rousing song, and tantalizing gifts. The tree was always trimmed with strings of Norwegian flags, shiny ornaments, and the woven paper heart baskets my grandfather made with us. The night, which lasted long, was the culmination of what seemed at times like unendurable anticipation. My mother and her sisters would start their preparations weeks before—cookies, breads, cured meat, and of course, fiskepudding.

This fiskepudding recipe is my grandmother's word for word, as are those for Julekake—Cardamom Raisin Bread—in *The Body in the Bog* and Norwegian Meatballs in *The Body in the Cast*.

When asked why Faith Fairchild doesn't appear more centrally in this book, I've flippantly answered that Faith would never go to Norway, because there would be nothing there for her to eat. While this may have been true some years ago—and on a trip in 1975, my husband did tell me he'd go mad if he ever saw another boiled potato—contemporary Norwegian cuisine whether in homes or in restaurants has changed, combining tradition with innovation to produce dishes even Faith would savor. Pillaging in the spirit, though not the manner, of their ancestors, you may now be served such hybrids as gravlaks millefeuilles, sushi-like marinated salmon tartares, or venison raviolis.

All this is fine with me—so long as there are always plenty of vafler.

Next to eating good dinners, a healthy man with a benevolent turn of mind, must like, I think, to read about them. —WM. THACKERY

Faith and I would add "and woman" to the phrase, but Thackery was definitely on to something. We enjoy reading about food. And for many of us, reading about food and murder is the real frosting on the cake. Why is the pairing of gastronomy and crime so seductive?

Dorothy Sayers delights us with her descriptions of Lord Peter Wimsey's meals, with perhaps the best title in the annals of culinary crime: "The Bibulous Business of the Matter of Taste." That short story describes a six-course dinner with the emphasis on the identification of the wines accompanying each course. Only the real Lord Peter is able to correctly name all of them. I like the breakfasts best and entertain fantasies of Bunter appearing at the door of my bed chamber, tray laden with tea, kippers, coddled eggs, and a rack of toast.

Meanwhile across the channel, Madame Maigret is taking excellent care of her husband, preparing traditional French dishes that Simenon writes about in mouth-watering detail. It is no wonder Maigret tries to get home for lunch so often. I would too if someone was whipping up coq au vin and a tarte à la frangipane (a particularly sinful custard pastry) for me.

On our own shores, we have Nero Wolfe, whose attention to food is as obsessive as his devotion to his orchids. He and Fritz Brenner, his chef, range over a number of cuisines in the pursuit of their art. Fritz is so gifted that he even makes milk toast "superbly". Why on earth would Archie ever look for his own apartment? Would you?

It would be simple to say that each author uses food as a way of characterizing each sleuth, a way of extending our knowledge of the kinds of people they are—and leave it at that. An idiosyncrasy perhaps? But it's more. We get hungry when we read these books and I'm sure the authors did too as they wrote. How could it be otherwise, given the emphasis they place on the joys of the table? Food is important. It makes a statement on its own. Whodunit is irrevocably joined to Whoateit.

Faith doesn't have a cook, nor do I. If we want something tasty, we have to make it ourselves; something, fortunately, both of us like to do. We hope you will enjoy these recipes and when you're ready to sit down to the fruits of your labor, prop a good mystery up in front of your plate!

Main Dishes

Vegetarian

Spanakòpeta
Greek Spinach Pie

2 packages of raw spinach
1 1/12 pounds feta cheese, chopped fine
1 large yellow onion, diced
6 large eggs
12 sheets of filo dough (Follow the package's instructions for handling)
1/2 pound unsalted butter
1/4 cup uncooked rice
Salt
Pepper

Beat the eggs in a large bowl. Wash, dry, and chop the spinach. Add it to the eggs and mix. Add the feta cheese, onion, and rice. Mix again. Add salt and pepper to taste, remembering that feta cheese is salty.

Preheat the oven to 350°. Melt the butter. Grease the bottom and sides of a 15"x10"x2" baking dish. Place 1 sheet of filo dough in the pan, so it covers the bottom and comes up the sides. Brush with melted butter and repeat with 4 more sheets. Pour the spinach/egg/cheese/onion mixture into the pan and spread evenly. Then add the remaining sheets of filo in the same manner. Be sure the top layer is well covered by melted butter. Pierce in several spots to allow steam to escape.

Bake for approximately 45 minutes. The top should be golden. Remove and let it sit for 5-10 minutes, cut into squares and serve. Serves 6 as a main course.

Cousin Luise's Linguini with Asparagus

1 medium-sized yellow onion
3 teaspoons minced garlic
4 tablespoons olive oil
2 tablespoons unsalted butter
12 ounces dried linguine
1 pound fresh asparagus
2 tablespoons water (from the pasta pot)
4 tablespoons white wine
2 tablespoons fresh lemon juice
4 tablespoons grated Parmesan cheese

Break off the woody ends of the asparagus. Asparagus breaks naturally at this point. Hold a spear and bend it. It will snap at the point where it becomes too tough. Then slice the spear diagonally into approximately 1-inch pieces. Set aside.

Boil water for the pasta while you are sautéing the onion and garlic in the oil and butter until golden. Cook the pasta according to the directions on the package and drain, reserving 2 tablespoons of the cooking liquid.

Add the asparagus to the onion/garlic mixture and cook for 2 minutes, stirring if necessary. Remove from the heat and add the water, wine, and lemon juice. Mix it with the pasta in a warmed bowl, adding the Parmesan cheese, salt, and pepper to taste—or you may serve it mounded on top of each pasta portion. Serve immediately. Makes 4 portions. The butter may be omitted and replaced by olive oil.

This is one of the best preparations for the first asparagus to appear in the spring, an elegant, yet simple recipe.

Pasta Frittata

1/2 pound capellini or spaghetti
1/2 cup plus 2 tablespoons grated Parmesan, Romano (or a combination of the cheeses)
2 tablespoons pesto
2 tablespoons olive oil
1 tablespoon unsalted butter
Salt
Freshly ground pepper
3 large eggs

Cook the pasta according to the instructions on the package, usually 3 minutes for capellini. Drain, place in a warmed bowl and add 1/2 cup grated cheese, 1 tablespoon olive oil, the pesto, a pinch of salt, and another of pepper. (Pesto, which you can make yourself in a blender or food processor, is a combination of fresh basil leaves puréed with garlic, olive oil, salt and pepper. Pine nuts and Parmesan are sometimes added. You can freeze pesto. You can also buy prepared pesto in specialty markets.) Mix well until all the strands are coated. Set aside to cool slightly for about 5 minutes. Beat the eggs in a separate bowl and add to the pasta, again, mix well. Heat 1 tablespoon olive oil with the butter in a frying pan. Add the pasta mixture, smoothing the top and sprinkling it with1 tablespoon grated cheese. Cook over medium heat until the bottom is nicely browned. Slide it on to a plate and flip it to cook on the other side, sprinkling the top with the rest of the cheese. You may also run it under the broiler until browned and not flip it or put the entire pasta mixture into a slightly greased casserole dish, baking it in a 350° preheated oven until firm. Cut in wedges. Serves four as a main course with salad or six as a first course or a side dish.

This is the recipe for making a frittata from scratch. As Faith tells the boys, you can make it using any kind of left over pasta as well.

If you happen to have some Fettucine Alfredo or pasta with Gorgonzola sauce left on hand—not likely in my house—eliminate the cheese.

Chicken, Beef, and Pork:

Chicken Stroganoff

2 pounds boneless, skinless chicken breasts
1 tablespoon unsalted butter
1 tablespoon olive oil
1 medium yellow onion
3/4 pound mushrooms
1 1/2 tablespoons unsalted butter
1 tablespoon flour
1 cup unsalted chicken broth
1/2 cup sour cream
1/4 teaspoon grated nutmeg
1/2 teaspoon paprika
Salt and pepper to taste
1/2 cup dry white wine

Cut the chicken into strips, removing any fat. Dice the onion and slice the mushrooms.

Heat 1 tablespoon butter and 1 tablespoon olive oil in a large frying pan or wok and stir-fry the chicken. When done remove to a warm plate.

While the chicken is cooking, melt 1 1/2 tablespoons of butter in a covered flameproof casserole. Add the flour and whisk to make a roux.

Slowly add the chicken broth and stir until smooth and thickened. Add the sour cream and seasonings, stirring well.

Sauté the onions and mushrooms in the same pan used for the chicken. You may need to add a bit more butter and olive oil.

When the mushrooms are nicely browned, add the mixture to the sauce and fold in. Deglaze the pan with the wine and add to the mixture. Finally fold the cooked chicken in, cover, and simmer. At this point the dish may be served or refrigerated, brought to room temperature, and reheated the next day. Serves 4-6.

Serve over egg noodles and sprinkle some finely chopped parsley on top of each portion.

Replacing the chicken with beef, the chicken broth with beef broth, and nutmeg with dried mustard brings the dish back to its original roots.

As with most recipes, these roots are gnarled. The dish is indisputably Russian and the name comes from Count Pavel Alexandrovich Stroganoff, who lived in St. Petersburg in the late 19th century. Some accounts state that the count's chef won a kind of Romanov bake-off with the recipe and named it in honor of his employer. Others ascribe its invention to the time the count spent in Siberia when his chef was forced to cut the frozen beef into thin strips before he could cook it. Still another states that the count had bad teeth and couldn't chew large chunks of beef. Whatever the name, it seems clear that the basic recipe was in use throughout Russia since the 18th century and may possibly have been cribbed from a 15th century Hungarian dish.

Whatever its true origin, Beef Stroganoff made its way to the United States and appeared early on in one of Faith's favorite cookbooks, *The Mystery Chef's Own Cookbook,* published in 1934. The author, John

MacPherson, whose motto was "Always be an artist at the stove, not just someone who cooks," was the host of a very popular radio show and appeared twice a week on one of television's first cooking shows on NBC in Philadelphia. He was originally from Britain and the term "Mystery Chef" was a nom de plume he assumed out of deference to his mother who was appalled that he had not kept what she called his "hobby" under "his hat." The name stuck and MacPherson says in his introduction, "Who I am doesn't matter. It is what I have to say that counts."—which could serve as a mantra for many chefs (and mystery fiction writers).

The Russian Tea Room in New York City served the dish and it was a favorite of James Beard's, who rightly pointed out that the secret was in cooking it quickly.

Serving Beef Stroganoff at a dinner party in suburban northern New Jersey when I was growing up there in the 1950's and 60's meant the hostess was someone with flair—slightly edgy international flair. She probably used La Choy chow mein noodles on top of her string bean and mushroom soup casserole instead of Durkee's French fried onions. She may even have added water chestnuts. She might, in fact, have been a relative of Faith's.

Boeuf Bourguinon (Beef Stew)

2 pounds chuck beef cut into large cubes
Flour
3 tablespoons olive oil
2 tablespoons unsalted butter
Salt and freshly ground pepper
1/3 cup cognac (optional)
1/4 pound bacon, diced
2 cloves garlic, minced
3 carrots, sliced into approximately 1" pieces
1 leek, the white part, cleaned and sliced
1 small yellow onion, diced (approximately 1 1/2 cups)
1/2 pound mushrooms, sliced
1 tablespoon minced parsley
1/2 teaspoon thyme
1/2 bottle Burgundy or similar red wine
Water

Dredge the beef cubes in flour (Faith does this the way her grandmother did by shaking the meat and flour in a brown paper bag). Melt the oil and butter in a large skillet and brown the meat. Sprinkle with salt and pepper. Pour the cognac, if being used, on top and carefully ignite. When the flames die down, transfer the meat to a casserole with a lid using a slotted spoon.
Preheat the oven to 350° F.

Add the bacon, garlic, carrots, leek, onion, and parsley to the skillet. Sauté until the bacon is slightly crisp and the onions, garlic, and leeks are soft. You should stir the mixture frequently.

Add the contents of the skillet to the meat.

Add the thyme, Burgundy and just enough water to cover the stew.

Cover and place the casserole in the center of the oven. Bake for 1-1 1/2 hours.

Serve with egg noodles and more parsley as a garnish. This dish tastes delicious the day it's made—let it rest for 10-15 minutes before serving—and even better if made a day ahead. Serves six.

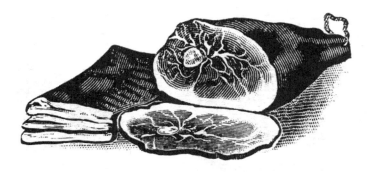

Smothered Pork Chops

4 one-inch thick center cut pork chops
1 1/2 teaspoons salt
1 teaspoon freshly ground pepper
2 teaspoons dried basil
1/2 teaspoon dried thyme
1/2 teaspoon dried rosemary
1 large garlic clove, halved
1/2 cup flour
1/3 cup vegetable oil
1 cup yellow onion, diced
1 medium green bell pepper, sliced
1 1/2 cups water

Rub the chops on both sides with the cut side of the halved garlic glove. Mix the salt, pepper, basil, thyme, and rosemary together. Generously sprinkle both sides of the chops, pressing the mixture into the meat. Cover loosely with waxed paper or plastic wrap and let stand in the refrigerator for 30 minutes. Remove and dredge the chops in flour. Heat the oil in a skillet large enough to hold all the chops. Brown on both sides, approximately 6 minutes on a side. Remove the chops to a warmed platter. Add the onions and peppers to the skillet and cook until soft, approximately 2 minutes. Add 2 tablespoons of the flour used for dredging and the water. Stir until the flour is completely dissolved. Return the chops to the pan and bring it to a boil. Cover, reduce the heat and simmer for 30-40 minutes

The pork will be very tender and the gravy delicious. Serve with rice.

Norwegian Meatballs

1/2 pound ground veal
1/2 pound lean ground beef
1/2 cup bread crumbs
1 egg, slightly beaten
1/2 teaspoon salt
1/4 teaspoon freshly ground pepper
1/8 teaspoon ground nutmeg
3 slices of salt pork (or slab bacon), 3 inches square, rendered

Sauce:
2 tablespoons butter
2 tablespoons flour
1 3/4 cups beef stock

Combine the meats, crumbs, egg, and seasonings into balls 1 1/2 inches in diameter, using as little pressure as possible. Cover and let stand for 1 hour.

Brown the meatballs in the pork fat.

In a separate pot, melt the butter and add the flour, whisking together to make a roux. Slowly add the stock, stirring constantly. Bring to a boil and add the browned meatballs. Simmer very low for 1 1/2 hours.

Serve over egg noodles and garnish with finely chopped parsley. Serves 4 to 6.

Coq Au Vin

1 roasting chicken cut into pieces
All-purpose flour for dredging
2 tablespoons olive oil
2 tablespoons unsalted butter
1/2 - 3/4 pounds carrots cut into 1" chunks
1 large yellow onion, peeled and cut into 8 wedges
1/2 teaspoon salt
1/2 teaspoon freshly ground pepper
1 1/2 cups red wine
1-1 1/2 tablespoons dried thyme

Dredge the chicken in the flour and brown, skin side down first, in the oil and butter. The best pan for this is a large, deep frying pan or a casserole large enough for a single layer of the chicken. After the chicken has been browned, add the carrots and onions to the pan, pour the wine on top, and season with the salt, pepper, and thyme. Turn the heat down slightly, cover, and cook until the chicken and carrots are done, approximately 45 minutes to an hour. The beauty of this dish is that even if it cooks longer, it still tastes wonderful—maybe even better. You can also add mushrooms or brown some bacon in the pan before adding the chicken, elements of the more traditional—and more complicated—coq au vin, but this one is sinfully quick, easy, and delicious. Serve with rice or egg noodles.

Pork Loin Stuffed with Winter Fruits

4 1/2 to 5 pound boned pork loin, center cut
1 large apple, peeled, cored, and cubed
Approx. 12 pitted prunes
Lemon juice from 1/2 lemon
Salt
Freshly ground black pepper
3 tablespoons unsalted butter
3 tablespoons vegetable oil
3/4 cup dry white wine
3/4 cup heavy cream

Ask your butcher to cut a pocket in the center of the pork loin and tie it at one-inch intervals or do this yourself at home. Toss the apple cubes with the lemon juice to prevent discoloration. Then, stuff, alternating pieces of apple and prune.

Preheat the oven to 350°. Put the butter and oil in a large casserole with a lid, a Dutch oven is good or Creuset-type cookware. Place the casserole on the top of the stove over medium heat. When the butter has melted, add the loin, turning it so that it browns evenly on all sides, seasoning with the salt and pepper as you cook it. Remove the fat with a bulb baster.

Pour in the wine and cook in the center of the oven for approximately an hour and a half. Use a meat thermometer to check to be sure it's done—but not overdone.

Place the loin on a heated platter and finish the sauce by first skimming off any fat produced during the cooking, then bringing the remaining liquid to a boil. Reduce the heat and add the cream, stirring constantly. Serve the sauce separately in a gravy boat.

A cranberry chutney or Scandinavian lingonberries go well with this dish. Serves six to eight.

Faith's Yankee Pot Roast

2 3/4 lbs beef bottom round, tied
1/3 cup olive oil
3 large carrots
3 medium onions
4 medium potatoes (Faith likes Yukon Golds)
3 cloves of garlic
1/2 tsp. thyme, more if using fresh
1 bottle Sam Adams lager, cream stout, or the equivalent
Salt and pepper

Brown the meat in the oil on all sides in a large casserole with a lid or Dutch oven.

Peel the carrots and potatoes. Cut the potatoes and onions into quarters and the carrots into 2 inch pieces. Mince the garlic. Layer the vegetables around the browned meat and add the thyme, salt, and pepper.

Pour the beer into the casserole and bring it to a boil, uncovered, on the top of the stove. After it boils, turn the heat off and place the casserole, covered in a preheated 350°oven. Cook for one hour, remove and let cool. Refrigerate overnight.

This tastes best when made a day ahead. Reheat in the oven and sprinkle with finely chopped parsley after arranging the sliced meat and vegetables on a warm platter. Serve the gravy separately. You may want to add some flour to thicken the juices on the top of the stove and adjust the seasoning.

NOTE: If you like your potatoes firmer, add them the next day before re-heating.

Pasta With Smoked Chicken and Summer Vegetables

4 pounds skinless, boned chicken thighs and/or breasts
2 cups diced carrots
2 cups diced zucchini
2 cups diced summer squash
1 cup diced yellow or red onion
1 diced red pepper
1 large sprig fresh rosemary
1 cup vinaigrette with 1 1/2 teaspoons fresh rosemary leaves
16 ounces tortellini, dried or fresh
5 ounces fresh chèvre
Salt
Pepper

Smoke the chicken on the grill, using hickory chips, apple wood, or any flavor you prefer. While it is cooking, dice the vegetables and make the vinaigrette, using your own recipe or Faith's—1 part balsamic vinegar to 3 parts olive oil plus 1/8 teaspoon Dijon mustard, pinch of salt and pepper. Add the rosemary leaves and shake well.

Steam the vegetables with the sprig of rosemary until soft, but not mushy. Remove the rosemary and toss the vegetables with the vinaigrette. Cook the tortellini according to the instructions on the package, drain and add the chèvre, mixing it thoroughly.

Cut the cooked chicken into bite-sized pieces and add to the tortellini. Add the vegetables and mix gently. Salt and pepper to taste.

This is a wonderful dish to bring to a party, as Faith does, garnishing it with nasturtiums from the garden. It should sit for about an hour and be served at room temperature. It can also be served over greens as a salad. Serves 8-10, at least.

SEAFOOD:

Asian Noodles With Crabmeat

8 ounces rice stick or cellophane noodles
8 ounces crabmeat, preferably fresh
1/4 cup scallions, sliced thin
1/4 cup dry white wine
2 tablespoons sesame oil

Following the directions for amount on the noodle package, bring a pot of water to a good boil. When the water is close to the boil, sauté the scallions. Add the noodles to the now boiling water. They will cook very quickly. Be sure to stir with a pasta muddler or a wooden spoon. As soon as you have started the noodles, add the crab and white wine to the scallions. Be careful not to overcook any of the ingredients. This is extremely fast food.

Drain the noodles and place a portion on four heated plates. Divide the crab/scallion mixture among them, adding a few uncooked sliced scallions on top. Serve immediately. Faith likes to serve steamed sugar snap peas or peapods with this dish. Serves four.

Seafood Risotto

2 tablespoons unsalted butter
2 tablespoons olive oil
1 small yellow onion, diced
1 1/2 cups Arborio rice
5 cups fish stock
2 cups small, cooked shrimp (shelled and deveined)
1/2 cup grated Parmesan cheese
8 ounces crabmeat
Parsley for garnish

Pour the both in a large saucepan and heat to a simmer.

While the broth is heating, melt the butter and oil in a pot (Faith likes a Creuset-type casserole). Sauté the onions until they are soft and add the rice, sautéing for 2 more minutes.

Using a ladle, add the heated stock approximately 1/2 cup at a time, stirring after each addition until all the liquid is absorbed. Whole Foods and other stores sell an excellent prepared fish stock if you do not have the time or ingredients to make your own.

When all the stock has been used, stir in the cheese and then fold in the shrimp and crab.

Serve garnished with chopped parsley. Serves six.

This is tasty with just the shrimp or crab. Heavenly with lobster.

Fiskepudding with Shrimp Sauce

SIGN IN A NORWEGIAN RESTAURANT: *Consumption of alcohol is forbidden unless accompanied by fish. All food is considered fish, except sausages. If sausages are ordered, may God forbid, sausages can be called fish.*

> *1 1/2 pounds white fish fillets (Haddock or a combination of Haddock and Sole is good.)*
> *1/2 cup light cream*
> *1 cup heavy cream*
> *2 teaspoons salt*
> *1 1/2 tablespoons corn starch*
> *1 tablespoon unsalted butter*
> *A buttered sheet of aluminum foil.*

Preheat the oven to 350° F.

Melt the butter and coat the inside of a mold such as a pudding mold or bundt pan. The mold should be large enough to hold six cups. Set aside.

Start boiling enough water, so that the mold will be covered by water 3/4 of the way up when placed in a large baking pan during cooking.

Cut the fish into small pieces, approximately one inch square.
Mix the creams together in a measuring cup with a spout or a pitcher.

Using the sharp blade on a food processor or a blender, blend the fish with the cream, one batch at a time. Don't overfill the blender or food processor bowl. Transfer the mixture to a bowl and add the salt and corn starch. Beat vigorously. It will be light and somewhat fluffy.

Transfer the pudding into the mold. Bang it on the counter top or floor and smooth the top with a knife. (Norwegian cooking tends to get physical.)

Seal the mold with the foil and place it in the baking pan. Pour in the boiling water and set the pan in the middle of the oven.

Cook for 1 hour. Take the mold from the pan. Let it stand for five minutes and unmold it on a decorative round platter. Drain off any liquid that may have accumulated. Spoon on some of the sauce and garnish with whole shrimp and parsley sprigs. Serve the rest of the sauce separately. Don't forget the lingonberries and boiled potatoes. Faith actually likes this dish, but uses steamed new potatoes or fingerlings instead of the boiled potatoes.

Serves 6.

NOTE: this can also be made in individual molds as a first course.

Shrimp sauce:

4 tablespoons unsalted butter
3 tablespoons flour
1 1/2 cups milk
1 thin slice onion
Salt
White pepper
1/8 teaspoon nutmeg
3/4 lb. uncooked small, fresh shrimp, peeled and deveined.

(The sauce can be made while the pudding is cooking.)

Melt the butter in a heavy saucepan. Add the flour, cooking for 2-3 minutes over low heat, stirring constantly. Increase the heat slightly and slowly add the milk, whisking or stirring constantly again. Add the onion slice and continue to stir for 5 minutes. Remove from the heat, discard the onion slice, add the nutmeg, salt and pepper to taste.

Return to the heat and add the shrimp, reserving some for the garnish. When the shrimp are pink, serve immediately. (You can make the sauce ahead and do this last step just before serving.)

Cook the shrimp for the garnish in rapidly boiling water until pink.

Lutefisk

No, this is not a joke. I am reproducing my cousin, Hege Farstad's recipe verbatim, so you will know what people like Garrison Keillor are talking about. But Hege's Lutefisk bears as much resemblance to the butt of all those jokes as, to paraphrase James Thurber, does Little Red Riding Hood's grandmother to the wolf—or the Metro-Goldwyn lion to Calvin Coolidge.

The best raw material for lutefisk is torsk, cod, split along the back bone before hanging to dry. The dried fish is usually cut into two parts and put into cold water for 6 to 8 days. The water is changed twice daily.

After the fish is removed from the water, the fish is peeled off the bones and put into lut, acid, which covers the fish. The lut consists of 35 grams of caustic soda and 7 litres of water. The fish should stay in the lut until soft, usually 24-48 hours, i.e., when soft enough to pierce a finger through it. The fish is then put into cold water for 2-3 days, changing water twice daily. The best way to keep finished lutefisk is to cut it into pieces and deep-freeze it.

To serve lutefisk (4 persons): 2-21/2 kg lutefisk, 1-2 spoonfuls of salt, and some water. Use a pan for poaching fish. Put water into the pan nearly up to the rack. Put the lutefisk on the rack when the water boils. The larger pieces first. Sprinkle salt over the fish, put the lid on, and boil until you can pierce the fish with a small baking pin, about 10-15 minutes. The fish must be served immediately!

Trimmings: Béchamel sauce with mustard added according to taste, fried bacon strips & fat, steamed green peas, boiled potatoes.

Serve lutefisk with Norwegian Beer and Linie Aquavit (NOT that Danish stuff) The Norwegian aquavit can only be called linjeakkevitt if it has been shipped in barrels to Australia and back, i.e., crossing the linje, the Equator, twice."

In this country, it may be more convenient to start with dry, unsalted cod. Norwegian-American cookbooks call for potash lye to make the lut.

Now you know.

Crab Cakes

1/2 cup mayonnaise, preferably Hellmann's
1 large egg, slightly beaten
1 tablespoon mustard, Dijon
1 pound fresh lump crabmeat, drained
1 cup crumbled saltines, 25-30 crackers
Vegetable oil

People have very strong feelings about crab cakes. They're like barbeque—beef or pork? Catsup based or mustard based sauce? With crab cakes, the debate starts with the crab —Maryland, Louisiana, and Maine devotees weighing in on one coast; Washington on another. Faith loves all and any crab, but is partial to Maine's Peekytoe crab, because she lives there. Then, breading, crackers, or potato as binding? Worcestershire sauce, Old Bay, Tabasco or all three to complement the crustacean? Celery? Onions? The following is the recipe Faith's family prefers after many happy trials. The Fairchilds like their crab cakes crabby with as few additions as possible.

Combine the mayonnaise, egg, and mustard. Mix well, then fold in the crabmeat and saltines. Faith puts the saltines between 2 sheets of waxed paper and rolls them with a rolling pin to crumble them. Let the mixture stand for about 3 minutes before shaping it into patties. This recipe makes 12 patties. Put them on a baking sheet, cover with waxed paper or Saran and refrigerate for an hour.

Fry the cakes in vegetable oil, about 3-4 minutes on a side until they are golden brown. Drain on a paper towel and serve. Do not fry the cakes in olive oil or any other oil with a strong taste. Faith uses canola oil.

For spicy cakes, add 1/2 teaspoon of hot sauce to the first three ingredients. Faith often serves her crab cakes with a dab of mayonnaise mixed with Old Bay seasoning to taste on the side.

The Body in the Big Apple

The Big Apple. Jazz musicians coined the city's familiar moniker in the Twenties. There were plenty of apples to pick from the tree, but only one "Big Apple", only one New York. If you had a gig there, you had it made. The ultimate destination.

Growing up in Northern New Jersey, I felt much the same. As teenagers, my friends and I used to say we lived "just outside the city", omitting the fact that we had to cross a state line to get there. At twelve, we were deemed old enough to take the DeCamp bus together to Port Authority—in the daytime. Armed with the small penciled maps my mother would draw, we'd head for Manhattan. One Saturday it would be museums. My cousin John convinced me to stand in line with him for several hours outside the Metropolitan Museum of Art to catch a sixty second glimpse of the Mona Lisa, on loan from the Louvre. It's the wait I remember best now, the mix of New Yorkers and out-of-towners, the jokes, the stories—holding places while people dashed off for a dog from the Sabrett's All Beef Kosher Franks stand. Another Saturday, we'd go from box office to box office on Broadway until we got tickets to a matinee (prices were much lower in the early Sixties). We saw everything from Richard Burton in Hamlet to Robert Preston in The Music Man. Sometimes we'd just wander, walking miles, entranced by the dramatic changes in the neighborhoods from one block to the next. Bialys and bagels gave way to egg rolls followed swiftly by cannolis as we moved Uptown.

No time of year was more magical than December and from the time I was a small child, there was always a special trip during the season to look at the Rockefeller Center tree and the department store windows. Other times of the year, my parents took us to the ballet, opera—the old Met with the cloth of gold curtain—, concerts, and special exhibits at the museums—the Calder mobiles like nothing anyone had seen before spiraling in the enormous spiral of the Guggenheim.

Then there were the restaurants—or rather one restaurant: Horn and Hardart's Automat. My 1964 Frommer's Guide advises:

"Inquire of any passer-by, and you'll be directed to one that's usually no more than a block-or-two away." Sadly, they have all disappeared and trying to explain the concept to my fifteen-year-old son—you put nickels in the slot next to the food you wanted, lifted the little glass door, snatched it out and watched the empty space revolve, instantly producing another dish—is well nigh impossible. Fortunately there are old movies. Just as difficult is describing the food—the superb, crusty macaroni and cheese with tiny bits of tomato, the warm deep dish apple pie with vanilla sauce, the baked beans in their own little pot. Most New Yorkers of a certain age wax nostalgic about automat food—the meat loaf! And a whole meal for $1.00.

My husband is the genuine article. A native New Yorker, born and bred in the Bronx. "The Beautiful Bronx" when he was growing up and we have a book of the same name to prove it. When he meets someone else from the borough, talk immediately turns to the Grand Concourse, the "nabe," and egg creams. Where he lived is now part of the Cross Bronx Expressway, but he can still point out his elementary school as we whiz past. New Yorkers are very sentimental.

And to continue in the manner of Faith Fairchild's sweeping generalizations, New Yorkers are also very rude, very generous, very funny, very stylish, very quirky, and very fast. Genetically, they have more molecules than most other Americans. The moment I step off the train or plane from Boston, in imitation my pace quickens, gaze narrows, and senses sharpen. Forget all those New York designer fragrances. The essence is adrenaline, pure and simple.

This book is a paean to New York City past, present, and future—written about the end of one very distinctive decade as the city is poised for another—and a new century at that. At the close of 1989, the last thing Faith imagines is that in a few years she'll be in exile—living in the bucolic orchards west of Boston. She'll keep her edge, though, will continue to read the Times and make periodic journeys back to Bloomies, Balducci's, and Barneys. always keeping in mind what the comedian, Harry Hershfield said, "New York:

Where everyone mutinies but no one deserts." 1900 or 2000—some things never change. It's a wonderful town.

The Body in the Bonfire

Jane Eyre arrives at Lowood and after breakfasting on burnt porridge, a "nauseous mess...almost as bad as rotten potatoes," she confronts her dinner, which she finds "to consist of indifferent potatoes and strange shreds of rusty meat, mixed and cooked together." She wonders within herself "whether every day's fare would be like this." Alas, yes. Geoffrey Williams and Ronald Searle entitled the chapter describing Nigel Molesworth's thoughts on "Skool Food" in *Down With Skool*, "The Piece of Cod Which Passeth Understanding." Certainly school food has never been associated with gastronomy, yet what we consumed in an abbreviated period of time in surroundings more likely to hinder than aid digestion is often remembered with something like affection.

My mother packed good healthy food for our lunches each morning, filling first our lunch boxes—now bringing astronomical prices on eBay—then brown paper lunch bags, as we entered adolescence and put away childish things. We ate sandwiches made from Pepperidge Farm, not Wonderbread. Carrot and celery sticks were lovingly wrapped in waxed paper. There was usually an apple or a banana. Wholesome plain milk stayed cool in our thermoses. Of course we longed for squishy bread, peanut butter and Fluff, chocolate milk, and store bought cookies. And, most of all, school lunches prepared by the cafeteria ladies: chicken a la King, franks and beans, American Chop Suey, Sloppy Joes, macaroni and cheese, lime and cherry Jello cubes with whipped topping, tapioca—"fish eyes and glue". Meat loaf. For lunch! With gravy and mashed potatoes! I looked at kids who nonchalantly plunked down their quarters and grabbed a tray each day and thought how lucky they were. And the food wasn't bad. A few times a year Mom would run out of bread or we'd be late or some other reason would put me in line with my own tray. The women were good, plain cooks, despite the persistent rumors that a kid once really had found part of someone's finger in the beans.

I would never have given a second thought to the school lunches if I'd had a lunch box like Gene Stratton-Porter's Elnora Comstock's in *The Girl of the Limberlost*. It was brown leather and when opened revealed

> a space for sandwiches, a little porcelain box for cold meat or fried chicken, another for salad, a glass with a lid which screwed on, held by a ring in a corner, for custard or jelly, a flask for tea or milk, a beautiful little knife, fork, and spoon fastened in holders, and a place for a napkin.

This was the other end of the spectrum from a tin lunch pail for high school girls in 1909. Reading the book at age nine or ten, it sounded absolutely perfect to me.

Meals and how we ate them at the college I attended hadn't changed much since Elnora's era when I entered in 1965. Food at college was too good. Each dorm still had its own kitchen—no food services—and the one I was in freshman year was renowned for its baked goods and presided over by a Mrs. Mallory named, "Dot"—not that we ever dared call her that to her face. There were piping hot popovers for breakfast, delectable lemon meringue pies, rich fudge cakes, flaky biscuits, and plenty of cookies. Collectively, we were "the freshman ton."

There was sit-down dinner every night—and we had to change into a skirt. We all kept a basic number that could be pulled on in a hurry in the front of our closets. Tuesday nights there were candles on the tables and you could invite a faculty member to dine. It was called gracious living and it was. Freshman waited on the tables wearing starched buttercup yellow aprons that stood up like butterfly wings at the shoulders. From Dot we learned what underliners were and what "Raise right, lower left" meant. Like Mansfield's "Mystery Balls", we had nicknames for everything and a perennial lunch time favorite was "Garbage Salad", a toothsome mélange of lettuce, tomatoes, hard boiled eggs, strips of ham, cheese, and anything else the kitchen had left over all hidden under a sweet dressing.

Times have changed and the notion of sitting down to dinner every night—taking that much time to eat—must seem to today's college students positively Victorian. But for us it was a chance to talk—and laugh. We had to stop for a while to break bread together. What could be better?

The Body in the Lighthouse

On the morning of September 11th, I was driving to a neighboring town for a reason I cannot now recall. I turned on the radio and heard what I first assumed to be a review of some disaster movie, but soon realized, fighting disbelief, was an actual news bulletin. I stopped at once and turned around.

What I do clearly remember from the short drive is what a beautiful day it was. At the moment I heard the news, I was looking at the Flint Farm fields stretched out on one side of the narrow road, the barn and farmhouse on the other—all under a cloudless blue sky. The farm dates back to the 1640's and Flints are farming it still. It will always be farmland; the family has given it to a trust. It will always be there. Growing up in New Jersey, approaching New York City so many times from across the river, I watched the Twin Towers go up and become a part of the familiar skyline. We thought they would always be there too.

Returning home, I ran into the house, unable to say anything to my husband except, "Turn on the television." We watched in horror as the second plane struck. Then, in what seemed like a very short time, saw the towers fall to earth. All day footage of two young women crouched behind a car appeared over and over again. They were clinging to each other looking up, then one pulled the other to her feet and they ran, shoeless, disappearing into the cloud of ash and debris. From their faces, you could tell they were screaming. There was no sound. I see their faces still.

There were no degrees of separation September 11th. Everyone knew someone affected. The first tragic news was that the mother and stepfather of one of the administrators at my son's school had been on the plane that went down in Pennsylvania. She has taken comfort from the knowledge that those passengers were able to prevent something even worse. A friend's brother didn't make it out; another friend's son did. We didn't try to make sense of it all, but went to a town vigil; prayed at our church, open all day and night; then finally attended the service and silent march the high school students organized. It was impossible to keep back the tears at the sight of all those youthful faces, quietly walking toward the bleachers at the football field. They could not, still cannot, know how different their lives will be.

And I was writing this book. I'd started it in July and was immersed in Faith's world. I wasn't able to get back there for many weeks. I talked with writer friends, some experiencing the same difficulty; others finding solace in their work.

Instead I read, cooked, cleaned closets—and we went to Maine. Especially that first weekend, it was the place we wanted to be. Away from CNN and the other stations for a while; the three of us together. As we drove north, every car displayed a flag. Turning off the turnpike onto the back roads to "Sanpere Island," every yard had a hand-lettered sign, more flags. It was Indian Summer. We sat watching the tides, the osprey still in her nest on the opposite point, and broke bread with friends, cherishing their company.

When I got back to this book, I rewrote the few post September 11th attempts I'd made. I'd lost the rhythm of Faith's life, just as my own had been so disturbed, but it came back. The book takes place in the summer of 2001, ending on September1st with a wedding. I think back to that summer and it now seems like some kind of Camelot, my own uncomplicated days very different from Faith's. As I wrote, I found myself giving her some of those moments as well—moments removed from the plot where she watches her children and husband, wanting to remember the secure, serene feeling forever. Just as many of us date things from before the Cuban Missile Crisis and before the assassinations of the Kennedys and Martin Luther King, we have another before. Yet, once back, this book was a joy to write, as they all are—especially at the end. I returned to it remembering the answer British mystery writer P.D. James gave when asked why crime fiction is so popular. She said, "These novels are always popular in ages of great anxiety. It's a very reassuring form. It affirms the hope that we live in a rational and beneficent universe."

This hope was affirmed in countless ways immediately following September 11th and continues to be in ways large and small all over the globe. This hope is my wish for you, dear reader.

Vegetables, Side Dishes and Salads

Polenta with Gorgonzola

3 cups cold water
1 cup yellow corn meal (called polenta in Italian specialty stores)
1/4 pound Gorgonzola cheese
1 tablespoon unsalted butter
Pinch of salt
Pinch of freshly ground pepper

Bring the water to a boil in a heavy saucepan or Creuset type casserole. Add the corn meal, preferably stone ground, in a steady stream, stirring constantly. Keep stirring for approximately 5 minutes as the polenta thickens. Faith uses a wooden spoon. Add the butter and cheese, stirring until they are melted, about one more minute.

Serve immediately or keep warm in the top of a double boiler, stirring occasionally. Serves six as a side dish.

Polenta is great. It can accompany a main dish fresh from the pot. It can also be spread out in a pie plate or 8-inch square Pyrex pan to cool, then cut into wedges or squares. These serve as a base for sauce or they may be fried in olive oil. Both are also delicious covered with roasted vegetables.

Many brands of instant polenta are excellent. Follow the directions on the box and again, add the butter and cheese at the last minute. Be sure the Gorgonzola is ripe, but not over ripe. If too ripe, it will give the polenta a slightly acidic taste.

Parsnip Puree

2 pounds peeled parsnips cut in 1/4" pieces
6 tablespoons unsalted butter, softened
1/2 cup heavy cream
1/2 cup chicken broth
2 tablespoons white horseradish, drained
Salt

Put the parsnips in a large saucepan and cover with water. Bring the water to a boil and simmer for about 10 minutes or until the parsnips are tender. Drain, return the parsnips to the pan and dry them over moderate heat. Shake the pan to thoroughly dry.
Heat, but do not boil, the cream, butter, and broth.

Puree the parsnips in a food processor with the warm cream, butter, broth mixture. Add the horseradish last. Increase the amount to taste.

Add salt to taste.

Serves 8.

This is a wonderful any time of year dish, but a staple of our family Thanksgiving. It is another of cousin Luise's great recipes.

Llapingachos with Salsa de Mali
Potato Cakes with Peanut Sauce

Llapingachos:

6 boiled potatoes, peeled and mashed
1/4 cup unsalted butter
2 yellow onions, finely diced
3 cups shredded sharp cheddar cheese
Salt
Pepper
2-4 tablespoons canola or other vegetable oil

Put the potatoes in a large mixing bowl and set aside. Fry the onions in the butter until translucent. Add the onions and cheese to the potatoes. Mix well and season to taste with salt and pepper. Make 12 patties, packing the potato mixture firmly, so the cakes do not fall apart when fried. Fry them in the oil until golden brown on both sides, approximately 4 minutes on a side. Set aside and keep warm.

Salsa de Mali:

2 tablespoons canola or other vegetable oil
1 yellow onion, finely diced
1 clove of garlic, minced
2 ripe tomatoes, peeled and chopped, or 1-1 1/2 cups canned diced tomatoes with its juice
1/2 cup chunky peanut butter
Salt
Pepper

Fry the onions in the oil until they are translucent. Add the garlic, tomatoes, and peanut butter. Stirring constantly, simmer the mixture until it is blended and heated through. Add salt and pepper to taste. Serve salsa de mali warm over the llapingachos.

This is a good buffet brunch dish, and you should figure on one potato (2 patties) per person. Faith likes to use Yukon Gold potatoes. Check ahead to make sure one of your guests is not allergic to nuts!

Inca and pre-Incan civilizations in Peru had more than 200 varieties of potatoes, which are native to the country and were "discovered" by Europeans when the Spanish conquistadors arrived. Potatoes are still a staple in Peruvian cuisine. Many organic farms and markets offer a wide variety of potatoes, some heirlooms—long forgotten varieties.

Experiment with these for fun. The sauce is also good with rice. It may be served in individual ramekins with a side salad for a luncheon.

Corn Pudding

2 cups fresh corn, cut from the cob
or
2 cups canned, frozen, or cooked corn
2 large eggs, slightly beaten
1 1/2 tablespoons unsalted butter melted
2 cups scalded whole milk
1 teaspoon sugar
1 teaspoon salt
1/8 teaspoon pepper

Preheat the oven to 325° F. Mix all the ingredients together and pour into a buttered baking dish. Set it in a pan of hot water, the water halfway up the sides of the dish, and bake until firm, approximately 45 minutes. Best with fresh corn, yet still a good side dish for a winter evening when elephant's eye high stalks are but a dream. Serves 4-6.

Salad with Warm Cheese Toasts

Chèvre—goat's milk cheese, a log or small disks
A baguette, French bread
Extra-virgin olive oil
Fresh or dried thyme
Mixed salad greens
Vinaigrette dressing

Preheat the oven to 350° F. Cut the bread into rounds, two for each portion. Faith likes to use a very thin bread called a Ficelle, which means "string" in French. Drizzle a small amount of olive oil on the top of each piece of bread. If you are using a log of cheese, cut approximately 1/3" rounds and place the cheese on the bread. Disks of goat cheese are available in specialty stores— Crottin de Chavignol, Rocamadour, and Picodon are several wonderful varieties. If you are using these, place one on each piece of bread. Drizzle a bit more oil on top of the cheese and sprinkle with a pinch of fresh or dried thyme.

Place the rounds on a baking sheet and bake for 5-7 minutes until the cheese is soft. While they are cooking, assemble the salads. Toss the greens with the dressing and divide among the plates. When the toasts come out of the oven, put them on top of the greens and serve immediately. This dish can serve as either a salad or first course.

A note on vinaigrette: Faith finds many recipes too tart for a number of her customers' palates and relies on a simple ratio—one part vinegar to three parts oil with a small amount of prepared mustard, salt, pepper to taste, and whatever herbs she has on hand. The vinegar can be red wine, balsamic, raspberry or any of the myriads available. The oil can be olive oil, nut oil, safflower oil, canola oil, or a combination.

Aleford Baked Beans

4 cups Great Northern beans or pea beans, dried
A pinch of salt
3/4 pound well streaked salt pork
3 tablespoons Dijon mustard
3/4 cup molasses
3/4 cup dark brown sugar
1 1/2 teaspoons fresh ground pepper
1 1/2 teaspoons salt
1 cup boiling water
1 large yellow onion

Soak the beans overnight and drain. Add a pinch of salt and enough water to reach two inches above the beans. Bring to a boil and simmer for an hour. Drain and reserve the liquid. The beans should be barely tender.

Preheat the oven to 400° F.

Scald the salt pork by letting it sit in boiling water for ten minutes. Cut two thin slices and place one in the bottom of your bean pot or casserole. Cut the other in small pieces and set aside. Score the rind of the remaining piece with a sharp knife and set aside also.

Mix the mustard, molasses, brown sugar, salt, and pepper with the boiling water. It's easiest to do this in a large glass measuring pitcher. Layer the beans in the pot with the pieces of salt pork and the molasses/sugar/mustard mixture, burying the onion in the middle.

Place the large piece of salt pork on the top, rind up and pour the remaining liquid over it. If there is not enough liquid to cover the beans, use some of the water you reserved when you drained the beans.

Be careful not to use too much liquid. You can always add more as the beans bake.

Put the lid on the pot, or cover on the casserole, and bake the beans at 400° F. for thirty minutes. Turn the temperature down to 200°F. and bake for six-eight hours, checking to see that the beans do not become too dry. Uncover the container during the last hour of cooking.

Baked beans were the Puritans answer to the crock-pot and provided them with a tasty meal during the Sabbath. The pot would be placed in the fireplace on Saturday morning, or handed over to the baker, who would call for it and place it in the community oven, usually in a nearby tavern. After cooking all day, the beans were ready for Saturday supper and Sunday breakfast. Traditionally Bostonians eat their beans with brown bread, but Faith has served them straight from the pot with everything from foccacia to corn bread. Beantown's pot is earthenware with a narrow throat, but this recipe tastes fine cooked in any deep casserole with a cover, such as a Dutch oven.

This makes a great many beans. For the next meal, add barbeque sauce, drop a poached egg on top, or give some to your neighbors.

Waldorf Salad

1 cup diced crisp celery
1 1/2 cups cored, but not peeled, diced Granny Smith apples
3/4 cup coarsely chopped walnuts
1/4 cup sour cream
1/4 cup mayonnaise
Pinch of salt
Freshly grated nutmeg to taste

Combine all the ingredients and mix well. Refrigerate for at least one hour before serving, then let it warm slightly. Serve as is or on a bed of greens. This recipe tastes best with a slightly tart apple, and Granny Smiths are also pretty with the green celery.
The original recipe was created by the maître d', Oscar Tschirky, not the chef—at New York's famous hotel, the Waldorf-Astoria. It called for equal parts of diced celery and apples combined with mayonnaise and served on lettuce. Walnuts were a later addition. Faith has altered it still more and on occasion replaces the walnuts with pecans, adds seedless green grapes or golden raisins and often a slight squeeze of lemon.

Serves six.

Cucumber and Dill Salad

2 large cucumbers
1/2 cup white vinegar
2 tablespoons sugar
2 teaspoons salt
1/4 teaspoon pepper
3 tablespoons fresh finely chopped dill
Dill sprigs for garnish

Slice the cucumbers as thin as possible, using a sharp knife or a food processor. One of my relatives uses a cheese slicer, an ostehøvel, "cheese plane," which was invented by the Norwegians. When used with cheese, it produces one, thin slice of gjetost at a time—possibly all one may want. If you have a slicer, it produces a cucumber slice one can almost see through.

Toss the cucumbers with 1 teaspoon salt, cover and refrigerate for at least 30 minutes. Drain the excess liquid.

Combine the vinegar, sugar, salt, and pepper and pour over the cucumbers. Add the chopped dill and mix to be sure it is evenly distributed. Return, covered, to the refrigerator.

Before serving transfer to a bowl with a slotted spoon and garnish with the dill sprigs. This salat is particularly good with fish (of course) and game. It is a koldtbord standard and will keep, refrigerated, for days.

Mini Zucchini Fritters

1 jumbo egg
1 1/4 cups milk
1 tablespoon melted unsalted butter
1 cup flour, sifted
1/4 teaspoon salt
Pinch of freshly ground pepper
1 shallot, minced
1 1/2 cups finely grated zucchini
2 teaspoons unsalted butter

Beat the egg, milk, and melted butter together and add to the flour, salt, and pepper. Mix until smooth, but do not overbeat.
Put the zucchini in a piece of cheesecloth or clean dishtowel and squeeze the excess liquid out. Sauté with the shallot in 2 teaspoons of butter until soft, about 3-5 minutes.

Add the zucchini mixture to the batter and drop the batter onto a well-greased, hot griddle in rounds, approximately 2 1/2 inches in diameter. Turn when golden brown. Makes 36 pancakes.

Straight from the griddle, these are a nice accompaniment to a main course, fanned on the plate with grilled meat or fish. For Faith's wedding hors d'oeuvres, spread the room temperature pancakes with salsa topped with a dollop of sour cream or smoked salmon, the sour cream and a twist of coriander or dill. The combinations are limitless, though, and these pancakes may be made ahead and frozen.

The Body in the Attic

It has been a long, cold winter in New England. The weather and the war have dominated, sapping our spirits and energy. It has been an indoor winter; only the heartiest venturing out for winter sports—or the newspaper. During these months and months of below freezing temperatures, burst pipes, and constant anxiety, I found myself thinking about—and turning to—comfort food and comfort books.

Comfort food is highly individualistic. One person's meat loaf is another's Mallomar. Often we associate comfort food with specific events or people. Where did we first eat it? Who made it? Try as I might, even with their recipes, I can't reproduce either my Aunt Ruth or Horn and Hardart's macaroni and cheese. Do taste buds alter with age? Or are some foods time and place specific?

When we were sick, we got ginger ale and "pink pills for pale people", children's aspirin. Progressing back to health, we advanced to cinnamon toast and/or beef bouillon on a bed tray with very wobbly legs. The thought of the flat soda, the toast, the soup still invokes the sickroom's happier qualities—mom all to myself, no school, and Betsy McCall paper dolls from the latest issue of the magazine. Either because we were extremely healthy children or because my mother came from a Scandinavian background where illness was not encouraged—"Let Nature take its course"— these sick days were rare and the comfort foods that accompanied them have acquired mythic powers.

Triscuits, Wispride cheese spread, and a glass of Almaden sherry were what awaited my father after work as he decompressed during that Cold War ritual known as the cocktail hour. Occasionally there would be Planters mixed nuts. There was a cachet, a glamour to these comestibles, forbidden treats only for adults. To nibble a Triscuit now is to commune with that long ago feeling of being a child watching and waiting for life to happen. Crackers and cheese and sherry—this was sophistication. Forget Nick and Nora Charles and their martinis—food, of course, never played a great role in *The Thin Man*—in New Jersey we knew what adult comfort food was.

Every once in a while, it's nice to spend a day in bed with a slight cold or a touch of the flu. "The pleasant land of counterpane", Robert Louis Stevenson called it. If you're very organized—and up to it—you can put a large thermos of cocoa, mint tea, or a bottle of ginger ale next to you to sip during a day that stretches out much longer than a workday. A box of crackers or Vanilla Wafers is all that is needed to complete the menu. Lovely if someone's around to bring chicken soup or cinnamon toast, but it's not necessary. A really good quilt is, as well as several down pillows. Then it's time to turn to comfort books.

Jane Austen and Agatha Christie are good comfort authors, because you can read them over and over again, never quite remembering the plots. Nancy Mitford—*Love in a Cold Climate*, *The Pursuit of Love*, *Don't Tell Alfred*—is ideal also, but because of the familiarity, the anticipated jokes, not the forgetting. In a similar fashion, Mary Roberts Rinehart's non-mystery Tish books are a panacea for all ills.

Another book for what ails you is Janet Gillespie's account of her childhood summers in Westport, Massachusetts, *A Joyful Noise*. It combines an appreciation of the natural world with an equal appreciation of her eccentric relatives. It's back in print now—from Partners Village Press—and earlier editions often turn up in library book sales—a great place for obtaining all sorts of comfort reads.

Mysteries are natural comfort books and if you feel a bug coming on, you can go to the library and bring a stack of them home, happy in the knowledge that if one doesn't grab you, there are a dozen more in the pile.

Vintage mysteries are perfect—the authors you may know—Dorothy Sayers, Arthur Conan Doyle, Wilkie Collins, the Baroness Orczy, and the ones you may discover—Craig Rice, Frances and Richard Lockridge, Joan Coggin, Elizabeth Dean, Phoebe Atwood Taylor, Constance and Gwenyth Little, Charlotte Murray Russell, and John Stephen Strange, many of which are available from the Rue Morgue Press in Boulder, Colorado.

And finally, there are children's books—definitely a misnomer when it comes to Madeleine L'Engle's *A Wrinkle in Time*, Jane

Langton's *The Fledgling*, Lucy Maud Montgomery's *The Blue Castle*. Harry Potter, or whatever your favorites may be—never forgetting Nancy Drew. These are books for a lifetime.

"Comfort" is the key word. Whether it's milk toast or Milky Ways; murder or mirth, may you be comforted.

The Body in the Snowdrift

Growing up, my taste in literature was catholic—I read anything I could get my hands on—but looking back, I've noted that my favorites fell into two diametrically opposed categories: books about large families and books about orphans.

Cheaper By the Dozen and its sequel, *Belles on Their Toes* recounted the authors' childhood growing up not far from my own home in New Jersey, with their parents, Frank and Lillian Gilbreth, the pioneers of time and motion study. The books are very, very funny, but it was the notion of being one of twelve that captivated me. The same with the lovely *All-Of-A-Kind Family* books by Sydney Taylor, a fictional account of five sisters—and eventually a brother— growing up on New York's Lower East Side in 1912. With so many from which to choose, there would always be a kindred sibling. Large families continue to fascinate me, although they are more rare these days, and it's easy to romanticize the pros and forget the cons (the Gilbreth's shared bathroom, for instance).

And then there were the orphan books—*The Little Princess*, by Frances Hodgson Burnett, Lucy Maud Montgomery's *Anne of Green Gables*, and wonderful *Daddy Long Legs* by Jean Webster—an Electra fantasy come to life, and it doesn't hurt to imagine Fred Astaire in the title role, as he was in the movie. As it turns out, Sara Crewe isn't the orphan she believes herself to be. Her father returns; Miss Minchin, the wicked headmistress, and the mean girls get their just deserts. I read and re-read my Scribners' copy, illustrated by Ethel Betts, weeping each and every time as Sara is forced into servitude. Montgomery's Anne Shirley and Webster's Judy Abbot were more feisty than Sara, but I realize now that what drew me to each heroine was her imagination. They were born storytellers and great believers in all kinds of magic. Although Lucy Maud Montgomery is best now remembered for her Green Gables girl, she wrote many other memorable books, including a series that featured Sara Stanley, "The Story Girl" (almost an orphan, mother deceased and an absent father). Sara entertains her cousins by telling them stories over the course of a summer—*The Arabian Nights*, Prince Edward Island style. Parents would have been in the way in these books; clipping wings that showed the readers how high they might also fly.

But back to families, which play such a central role in *The Body in the Snowdrift*. The idea for this book started with the notion of a family reunion. Tom's family was a natural—large enough and filled with people I'd thought about over the series, but had never presented. It was time.

In *Anna Karenina*, Tolstoi wrote "Happy families are all alike; every unhappy family is unhappy in its own way." I've never agreed with this. For one thing, it makes the happy families sound so boring and as the years pass, it seems to me that the reverse is true. Especially if you add the word, "reunion" to the sentence in place of "family." The Fairchilds gather for what Dick Fairchild fondly believes will be a happy family reunion, but Faith knows better. She's watched her husband's siblings repeat their time honored familial roles over and over again, unable to get unstuck. It's a happy family, but an unhappy reunion—like so many that start out well intentioned and run into obstacles. I like to think that in the ensuing years, the Fairchild family gets unstuck, but not unglued, and perhaps this is a good goal for every family whatever size.

Food helps—family reunion, ritualistic food. Marian Fairchild's cole slaw, Aunt Susie's cake. We spend Thanksgiving with my husband's family and without Aunt Lil's cranberry mould, plus the little pigs in a blanket the children devour before the main event, the universe would wobble. For years, my family celebrated Christmas Eve in the traditional Scandinavian manner. My mother, one of seven, and her sisters would start preparing weeks in advance. The night itself is preserved in memory as a joyous celebration of family—with so many cousins I could imagine myself a Gilbreth.

But time takes people away—moving too far to come back, adopting a spouse's customs, or permanent loss as one generation gives way to the next. We will never get used to those empty places at the table. New traditions spring up; new kinds of reunions.

We make our own families, perhaps from the family we're born into, perhaps from the friends we love and if we're lucky, from both.

POSTSCRIPT: As I was looking up some of these books to see whether they were still in print on the Internet, I was interested to see that *Cheaper By The Dozen* was being paired with *All-Of-A-Kind Family* as a special. I had expected to find Frank and Ernestine Gilbreth's book, because of the recent movie (which bears no resemblance to the one with Clifton Webb and Myrna Loy in the early 1950's, and very little to the book), but finding Sydney Taylor so prominently featured was a joy. Family stories—sagas—will never go out of fashion.

NOT-JUST-FOR-BREAKFAST DISHES

Blueberry Muffins

2 1/2 cups flour
1 cup sugar
2 tablespoons baking powder
3/4 teaspoon salt
1 teaspoon nutmeg, preferably freshly ground
3/4 teaspoon cinnamon
2 large eggs
1 cup milk
3/4 cup unsalted butter melted
2 cups blueberries
Butter for greasing

Preheat the oven to 400° F. Sift together the dry ingredients: flour, sugar, baking powder, salt, and spices. Lightly beat the eggs, milk, and melted butter together. Add this to the dry ingredients and mix. Fold the blueberries into the batter and fill each cup in the muffin tin completely, not 3/4. Makes 2 dozen muffins.

Doughnut Muffins

from Lily's Cafe, Stonington, Maine

3 cups all-purpose flour
1 tablespoon baking powder
1/2 teaspoon baking soda
1/2 teaspoon salt
10 tablespoons unsalted butter, softened
1 cup minus 1 tablespoon granulated sugar
2 large eggs
1 1/2 cups plain low-fat yogurt
1 teaspoon vanilla

Preheat the oven to 350° F. Cream the butter and sugar together in a large mixing bowl until fluffy. In a separate bowl, mix the dry ingredients. Add the eggs to the butter mixture one at a time until mixed well together. Add the vanilla and mix, then add the dry ingredients, alternating with the yogurt. Divide the batter among twelve greased muffin cups and bake for 15-20 minutes or until a toothpick comes out clean.

While the muffins are cooling, melt one stick of unsalted butter and set aside. Combine 1/2 cup of sugar and 2 teaspoons of cinnamon. After the muffins are cool, dip the tops into the melted butter, then into the sugar and cinnamon mixture.

Southern Corn Bread

1 1/2 cups stone ground corn meal
3 tablespoons flour
1 tablespoons sugar
3 teaspoons baking powder
1/2 teaspoon salt
1/2 teaspoon baking soda
1 cup buttermilk
2 eggs, well beaten
4 tablespoons dripping

Preheat the oven to 350°. Combine the dry ingredients and stir in the wet. Pour the mixture into a lightly buttered 8" square pan and bake for 40 minutes, checking after 30. This is a dense, chewy cornbread and serves 6-8. The batter may also be fried in a large pan on top of the stove, flipping it over so both sides are crunchy.

Big Apple Pancakes

3/4 cup plus 2 tablespoons milk
2 tablespoons unsalted melted butter
1 egg
1 cup all-purpose flour
2 teaspoons baking powder
2 tablespoons sugar
1/4 teaspoon salt
1/4 teaspoon cinnamon
1 Empire apple peeled, cored and cut into thin slices, halved

Put the milk, butter and egg into a mixing bowl and beat lightly. Sift the dry ingredients together and add to the liquid ingredients, stirring just enough to mix. Add the apple slices and stir. Cook on a griddle or in a frying pan, making sure that the apple slices are evenly distributed in the batter. Makes 16 four-inch pancakes.

Serve with warm maple syrup—they don't need much.

Cardamom Raisin Bread

1 quart milk
1 1/2 cups sugar
1/2 cup butter
1 tablespoon ground cardamom
2 cakes compressed yeast or two packages of yeast granules
1 teaspoon salt
1 package seedless raisins
1 package golden or Muscat raisins
2 eggs beaten
12 cups flour (approximately)

Topping: 1 egg yolk, 1 teaspoon vanilla, 1 tablespoon sugar, mixed together

Heat milk and sugar, add butter and cardamom. When butter has melted, cool mixture to lukewarm. Add and dissolve yeast. Add salt, raisins, peel, if used, and beaten eggs. Work well together and add enough flour to make a firm but elastic dough. Cover dough and let stand in a warm place until doubled in bulk. Knead well and form into two round loaves—or four standard sized bread loaves. Place on greased pie tins, or loaf pans and let rise until doubled again.

Bake at 350° for 1 hour. Brush loaves with egg, vanilla mixture when they come out of the oven.

Once you've made it, you'll get the knack. It needs to rise for a long time and you also have to watch that the top doesn't get too brown or burn in the oven. You may have to cover it with foil near the end. You can also make the dough in a braid.

This Cardamom Raisin Bread is a Norwegian recipe from the real author's grandmother. We've always made it for Christmas. In Norwegian, it's called "Julekake," "Christmas Cake. I now make it all year round.

"The Annie" Breakfast Sandwich

2 large eggs (per person)
1/4 cup crumbled feta cheese
1 generous handful loosely packed fresh spinach, stemmed
2 slices tomato
Freshly ground pepper
Unsalted butter
2 slices of grilled or toasted sourdough bread

Beat the eggs and stir in the cheese, spinach, and a pinch of pepper.

Butter the bread and set aside on a warm plate.

Scramble the egg mixture in a nonstick frying pan.

Place the tomato slices on the bread and mound the filling on top. Cut the sandwich in half and serve immediately. Good with rye also.

Kyra Alex of Lily's Cafe in Stonington, Maine names many of her sandwiches and other dishes for friends—Ethel's Pulled Pork, Darrell's Muffaletta, Cecil's Chicken, and, in this case, Annie. I think of it as my sister, Annie's, though.

Patriot's Day Pancakes

1/2 cup milk
2 tablespoons melted butter
1 egg
1/2 cup sour cream
1 cup flour
2 teaspoons baking powder
4 tablespoons sugar
1/2 teaspoon salt
1/4 teaspoon vanilla
1/2 cup raspberries
1/2 cup blueberries

Mix the milk, melted butter, egg, and sour cream in a bowl until smooth.

Sift the dry ingredients together in a separate bowl and add all at once to the liquid ingredients. Stir until moistened. The batter will be a bit lumpy. Add the vanilla and stir again. Fold in the berries.

The pancakes cook more evenly if you can find blueberries and raspberries of approximately the same size.

Cook on a hot griddle over medium heat. Serve immediately with a dusting of powdered sugar. (Some people also like butter.)

Makes 18-24 pancakes depending on size. You may also wish to add more fruit, but not too much or the pancakes get mushy.

Delicious with syrup or without.

Vafler—Sour Cream Waffles

2 eggs
1 cup sour cream
1/3 cup melted butter
1/8 teaspoon vanilla
3/4 cup milk
1 cup flour
3 tablespoons sugar
1/2 teaspoon baking powder
1/4 teaspoon salt

Beat the eggs and add the sour cream, whisking well together, then add the butter, vanilla, and milk, whisking again. Add the dry ingredients and stir. The batter may seem thinner than your usual waffle batter.

Cook in a preheated waffle iron; one that makes heart shapes is all the better. The finished waffle should be nicely browned. Makes approximately 2 dozen three-inch heart shaped waffles.

Vafler are served room temperature with jam and butter, or sometimes powdered sugar. Never maple syrup. To vary the flavor, add 1/8 teaspoon of cardamom instead of the vanilla occasionally.

The Body in the Ivy

 I wrote the first Author's Note at the end of *The Body in the Cast*, the fifth in the series, to explain why I was including recipes for food mentioned in the book and why I hadn't done so earlier. Since that first note, I have enjoyed stepping from behind the curtain and speaking directly to readers. In the case of this particular book, I want to make it clear that, although some of my characters weren't happy at Pelham College, this in no way reflects my opinion of similar institutions of higher learning. I attended a women's college during roughly the same time period described here and have been forever grateful both for the education I received and the lasting friendships I made—and for all sorts of other experiences, which have provided such rich fodder over the years for conversation.

 My class was a class on the cusp. When we arrived as freshmen, the rules were essentially unchanged from a time when young women were thought to need stringent regulations lest they wittingly or unwittingly run amok. By the time I graduated, sign-outs had been abolished, as well as many of the other carry-overs (current students at my alma mater are the most shocked by the fact that we couldn't have cars on campus, "How did you get anywhere?"). The dress I wore for my admissions interview was demure—a navy blue wool cap-sleeved sheath with a white linen collar. It ended exactly in the middle of my knee. By senior year, we were all in micro-minis and bold Marimekko prints from Finland. We wore our hair as long and as straight as possible, forsaking the rigid rollers, the worst had brushes inside, that we slept on in our teens for ever more bizarre techniques. We'd ask a friend to iron our locks, for example. One girl had her fifteen minutes of fame as the inventor of a method that involved using your own head as a giant roller, swirling the wet hair close to the skull and securing it with clips until it dried, almost perfectly straight. We wanted to look—and sound—like Joni Mitchell and Joan Baez.

 I loved those four years. My classroom experiences where every woman had a voice and used it empowered us. It was all right to be smart. We had wonderful mentors in both female and male professors. There was an extraordinary greenhouse and yes, the Century Plant did bloom our freshman year, providing us with a symbol of both the transitory and enduring nature of life. We wouldn't be around for the next show of blossoms, but another group of young women probably not unlike us, would.

The student body today is a diverse one in all ways—a vast improvement. Accents are not erased, nor students assigned rooms on the basis of religion or ethnicity.

"Gracious Living" was stifling at times, but even then we treasured those sit-down dinners (most of us kept a "dinner skirt" within easy reach, one that could be donned quickly after shedding our jeans). We were forced to stop whatever we were doing, break bread, and talk to each other. Having been used to family dinners, I grew to treasure my new family, a family of friends. And over forty years later, the topics of our conversations have changed, but not the act of conversing—especially the helpless laughter and on occasion, the tears. When I applied to college, the mother of a friend of mine encouraged me to apply to a woman's college saying, "You will mostly be with women all your life, so you need to learn how wonderful and strong they are." I didn't really understand what she was getting at then, but I know it now, just as Faith does. I hope I've been able to convey how important her female friendships are to her, as well as the close tie she enjoys with her sister.

As I wrote this book, which depicts the way a group of friends is destroyed by the pathology of one member, I was concerned that readers might assume, incorrectly, that I thought this is what happens when you isolate women in a college setting, or any other one, for that matter. This is why I made such a point at the end of the book of rekindling the friendships that were so horribly disrupted by Prin's actions. I like to think that perhaps Barbara Bailey Bishop sells her island and finds someplace on the mainland where they all gather again in the future—with Faith in the kitchen, of course.

The Body in the Gallery

Food and Art. Food in Art. The Art of Food. Whatever the formulation, the two words go together and have throughout history. Friezes in the tombs of the pharaohs depict food in all forms from cultivation to preparation to feasting. A wall painting from Herculaneum c. 50 A.D. shows four luscious peaches and a simple carafe half filled with sparkling clear water. Nimble Norman needle workers depicted steaming cauldrons and early shish kabobs in the Bayeux tapestry. Bruegel invites us to sit down with the revelers at the Peasant Wedding and share the abundant cakes and free-flowing ale. 17th century Dutch still lifes conveyed the quality of the artist's patron's table—plentiful game, rare fruits and gleaming plate in such exquisite detail that we are tempted to pluck a grape from the canvas. Chardin's 18th century works such as Kitchen Still Life and Back From Market show simpler, but equally appetizing fare—crusty bread and a poulet for the pot.

The Impressionists were interested in painting food—Cézanne's fruit, Manet's asparagus, and both Manet's and Monet's Dejeuner sur l'Herbe. Manet's was a pretty skimpy picnic, a few cherries, some other fruit, a roll or two compared with Monet's generous spread that included roast chickens, bottles of wine, fruits, bread, and a large pâté en croute. Besides immortalizing food in paint, the Impressionists also liked to cook it. One of my favorite books is Claire Joyce's *Monet's Table: The Cooking Journals of Claude Monet*. Beautifully illustrated, it is as much a feast for the eye as its recipes are for the mouth. When Monet moved to Giverny, he painted the dining room a sunny yellow and put blue and white tiles in the kitchen that overlooked the gardens, which included an extensive kitchen garden. The artist entertained his friends and family frequently, recording his recipes and some of theirs—Cézanne's bouillabaisse, Millet's petits pains.

I have recently discovered another book, *The Artist's Palate, Cooking With the World's Greatest Artists* by Frank Fedele, which has recipes from Michelangelo (Based on three of his existing grocery lists: bread, grapes, anchovies, tortellini, spinach, fennel, "mellow wine"), Matisse (Soupe de poissons, French fish soup), Mary Cassatt (Chocolate caramels), Jackson Pollock & Lee Krasner (Bread and cheese hominy puffs), Andy Warhol(A traditional Thanksgiving dinner), Grant Wood (Strawberry shortcake), and Red Grooms (Confetti egg salad) created by chefs well known for their artistry in the kitchen: Mario Batali, Ming Tsai, André Soltner, David Bouley, and Jean-Georges Vongerichten. Fedele's descriptions of the artists' culinary predilections, based on interviews with friends and family where possible, are fascinating. According to Al Hirschfeld's wife, "Everyone from Charlie Chaplin to Whoopie Goldberg has tasted it!"—Hirschfeld's famous Caviar with Rice Crackers. And Louise Bourgeois's eats the same meal every Sunday: Linguini with American cheese, served in a frying pan, after which she has coffee ice cream served in the same pan. Both accompanied by a soda. The book is sumptuously illustrated with photographs of the artists and reproductions of their work.

Yet, when it comes to cookbooks paired with art, it's two older ones I love the best. The first is *Picasso and Pie*, a slim volume that you can still find on the Internet. It was published by Lynne Thompson in 1969 and is a collection of recipes that were served at The Blue Hill Buffet in Blue Hill, Maine, part of the Maine Gallery in Blue Hill. Perhaps it's the title that enchants—pairing a great artist with a great dessert—but recipes like Blueberry Ambrosia also stand the test of time. This is a fruit soup with its roots in Scandinavia that is served very cold with whipped cream. The Buffet's Blue Hill Fudge Cake was the 1951 New York Times cake of the year and there's also a great fish chowder recipe with instructions to serve it properly with Pilot Biscuits.

The other book, *The Art Lover's Cookbook*, was published in 1975 by The Summit Art Center in Summit, New Jersey, as a fundraiser for the center, which started in 1933 when a small group of artists began meeting in one of their studios to paint and discuss art. After various incarnations, the center moved into its own architecturally striking building in 1973 with plenty of studio and exhibition space. It's still going strong. My mother, who was a painter, was an active member. Each artist provided one or more recipes for the cookbook and each page is a work of art, illustrated and lettered by the artist. A pen-and-ink sketch of a Greek port accompanies Hella Bailin's Tzatziki; my mother's Norwegian Fish Pudding (it's like a mousse) features a delicate pencil drawing of several fish. Jane Crow entitled her offering, "Beef in Beer or More Time in the Studio" and pictured herself before her easel, a smile on her face. A note on fundraising cookbooks: they are addictive. I have them from organizations ranging from churches and libraries to service organizations and historical societies. Besides recording regional recipes that are disappearing all too fast, they provide an intimate glimpse of a group—usually women—and the way food brings people together. My current favorite is: *Food To Die For, A Book of Funeral Food, Tips and Tales*. It's the creation of The Southern Memorial Association (www.gravegarden.org/cookbook.htm), which uses the profit to preserve and manage the historic Old City Cemetery in Lynchburg, Virginia.

I can't conclude these thoughts on Food and Art without mention of what I call the "Food Museums," my favorites being the Food Halls at Harrods in London and Fauchon in Paris. Food is displayed to appeal to the eye first and foremost. The offerings are positively Lucullan and over the top. If it's "Location, location, location" in real estate, then it's "Presentation, presentation, presentation" in cooking. You have only to watch Iron Chef to learn that. (My mother the artist always served food on white plates, so the colors and textures wouldn't fight with a pattern.)

And finally a nod to some additional modern artists. Andy Warhol's Campbell Soup cans tapped into a visual iconic symbol of American life, but they also played upon a gustatory one. Few of us do not have strong, positive associations with that "Mmm, Mmm Good" tomato soup or chicken noodle flavor from our childhoods.

Wayne Thiebaud's marvelous paintings of cakes, ice cream, pastries, hot dogs are visually arresting, but make our mouths water too—like all the other artists starting with the unknown Egyptian sketching baskets of grain and even earlier, the Lascaux cave paintings of bison and other game. I always think of the old Automat when I look at Thiebaud's rows of slices of cakes each on a plate. They remind me of the walls of delicious offerings behind the little glass doors just waiting for our quarters.

Edward Weston's black and white photographs of vegetables, particularly peppers, are sensual delights. Maine photographer, David Klopfenstein, turns pears into evocative portraits that challenge us to place them in a particular era. The same is true of Isabelle Tokumaru whose shimmering, jewel-like oils of cherries, plums, pears, and satsumas evoked the following words from her writer husband, Joe Coomer: "Here is the perpetual fruit you desire and never tire of eating." This sentence is the perfect description for all the works of art I've mentioned.

Roman mosaics, medieval tapestries, Indian temple sculptures, Japanese prints—I've barely scratched the surface in this short note. The pairing of food and art is natural; the consumption of both, a necessity.

JUST DESSERTS

Cambridge Tea Cake

1 cup unsalted butter
1 1/2 cups sugar
5 large eggs
1 1/2 teaspoon mace
Pinch of salt
2 cups sifted cake flour

Grease and lightly flour a loaf pan, approximately 9 inches by 3 1/2 inches and set aside.

NOTE: Do not preheat the oven. This cake goes into a cold oven. Cream the butter with the mace and salt. Gradually add the sugar and beat until fluffy.

Add the eggs, one at a time, beating well in between.

Stir in the flour and mix. The batter should be very smooth.

Fill the pan and place the cake into the oven. Turn it to 300°.

Check with a cake tester or broom straw after 1 1/2 hours. It should be done or close to done.

Try toasting slices of Cambridge Tea Cake and topping them with fresh fruit, ice cream, or both.

Glad's Brownies

4 squares unsweetened chocolate
1 1/2 sticks unsalted butter
2 cups sugar
3 large eggs
1 teaspoon vanilla
1 cup sifted flour
1 cup dried cherries
1 1/4 cup chopped walnuts
1 cup chocolate chunks or chips (milk or semi-sweet)

Preheat the oven to 350°. Grease and lightly flour a 13"x 9" pan. Melt the chocolate squares together with the butter. Cool it slightly and beat in the sugar, eggs, and vanilla. Stir in the flour.

Mix well, then add the cherries, walnuts, and chocolate chunks or chips. Put the batter in the pan and bake for about 35 minutes. Be careful not to over bake. Cool in the pan and serve. Makes a very generous1 1/2 dozen.

You may vary this recipe by substituting dried cranberries, golden or dark raisins for the cherries and pecans for the walnuts. Attributed in the book to Faith as a child, it is actually the creation of the author's dear friend, Gladys Boalt of Stormville, New York.

Red Velvet Cake

2 1/4 cups sifted cake flour
2 tablespoons unsweetened cocoa powder
1 teaspoon baking soda
1 teaspoon baking powder
1 teaspoon salt
1 1/2 cups sugar
1/2 cup unsalted butter at room temperature
2 large eggs
1 cup buttermilk
2 ounces (1/4 cup) red food coloring (for a very deep red)
1 teaspoon vanilla
1 tablespoon white vinegar

Preheat the oven to 350°.

Grease and flour two 9-inch round cake pans.

Sift the flour, cocoa, baking soda, baking powder, and salt together. Set aside.

Cream the sugar and butter.

Add the eggs, one at a time, beating well after each addition.
Add the flour mixture to the butter and sugar, alternating with the buttermilk.

Add the food coloring, vanilla, and vinegar. Beat well.

Bake for approximately 30 minutes or until a toothpick or broom straw comes out clean.

Cool on a cake rack.

Frosting:

8 ounces cream cheese at room temperature
1/2 cup unsalted butter at room temperature
1 box (1 pound) sifted confectioners' sugar
1 teaspoon vanilla

Cream the butter and cheese. Add the sugar, beating until the mixture is fluffy. Add the vanilla and beat some more.

Fill and frost the cake.

You may add chopped pecans or walnuts to the frosting or use them on top of the cake. Some cooks like to sprinkle coconut on top.

Serves 6-8. These also make lovely cupcakes.

Aunt Susie's Cake

1 box good quality yellow cake mix
4 eggs
3/4 cup canola or other vegetable oil
1 (11 ounce) can Mandarin oranges packed in juice
For the frosting:
1 small package instant vanilla pudding
1 large (20 ounce) can crushed pineapple packed in juice
1 large container Cool Whip or other whipped topping

Combine the cake mix, eggs, oil, and oranges (including juice) in a bowl. Mix according to the directions on the box. Pour into 3 round cake pans and bake at 350° for approximately 25 minutes.

Remove from the pans and cool on cake racks while you make the frosting.

Drain the pineapple, reserving the juice. Mix the juice and the instant pudding together. Add the Cool Whip and drained pineapple. Mix. Spread some of the frosting between the layers and use the rest on the top and sides of the cake.

This recipe comes from Linda Gronberg-Quinn, who was the high bidder for a chance to put a favorite recipe in one of my books at the Malice Domestic Convention's auction for the benefit of Maryland's John L. Gildner Regional Institute for Children & Adolescents. Her husband's Aunt Susie, Susan Houston, is a "prototypical Southern lady" writes Linda, and "we are constantly amazed at how wonderful her cooking tastes even though it is a seemingly simple recipe." This is the dessert Aunt Susie brings to a Pig Pickin', where after picking the succulent meat from the roast pig, people always save room for her cake. Whatever your main course, you'll save room for this layer cake too. Thank you, Susie and Linda.

Chocolate Bread Pudding

5 thick slices of chocolate bread, cubed
4 large eggs
1 1/2 cups milk
1 1/2 cups half and half or light cream
1/4 cup white sugar
1 teaspoon vanilla
Pinch of salt
Butter to grease the pan
1 cup dried cherries
1 cup semi-sweet chocolate morsels

Mix the eggs, milk, half and half, sugar, vanilla, and salt together. Faith likes to pulse this in a blender, which makes it easy to pour over the bread cubes.

Put the bread cubes in a large mixing bowl and pour the egg mixture over them. Use the palm of your hand to gently push the bread into the liquid to make sure it absorbs evenly. Cover with plastic wrap and refrigerate for at least 30 minutes.

Butter a Pyrex-type baking pan, approximately 12" x8". Set aside.

Preheat the oven to 350°.

Mix the cherries and chocolate chips together in a small bowl.

Put a layer of the bread mixture in the pan, sprinkle the cherry/chip mixture over it, and cover with the remaining bread mixture. Again, use the palm of your hand to press down, so the ingredients are evenly distributed.

Bake for 40 minutes.

Serve warm with vanilla ice cream or frozen yogurt.

This is a very rich dessert and this recipe will serve 12 easily.

Neither Faith nor I have ever met a bread pudding we didn't like. It's comfort food. Many bakeries make chocolate bread. *When Pigs Fly*, the bakery company mentioned in the text is based in Wells, Maine, but their breads—including the chocolate bread—are sold at many Whole Foods and other markets. They also sell the bread—you bake it in your own kitchen for the last 30 minutes—online at www.sendbread.com. They also sell a kit to make the chocolate bread.

Harvard Squares

1 cup unsalted, softened butter
3/4 cup firmly packed brown sugar
3/4 cup white sugar
2 large eggs
1/2 teaspoon vanilla
2 1/4 cups unsifted flour
1 teaspoon baking soda
1/2 teaspoon salt
1 cup chocolate chips
1 1/2 cups peanut butter chips

Cream the butter, then add the sugar and beat until fluffy. Add the eggs and vanilla, mixing well. Combine the flour, salt, and baking soda, then add to the batter. Combine the chocolate and peanut butter chips. Stir them into the batter.

Spread the batter evenly onto a well greased jellyroll pan, approx. 15 1/2 inches by 10 1/2 inches.

Bake in a preheated 350° oven until golden brown, about 25-30 minutes.

Cool in the pan, then cut into squares. Makes 48 squares.

You may substitute butterscotch or other kinds of chips for the peanut butter chips.

Comfort Cookies

2 sticks unsalted butter at room temperature
1 cup brown sugar
3/4 cup white sugar
2 large eggs, slightly beaten
1/2 teaspoon vanilla extract
2 1/4 cups all purpose flour
1 teaspoon baking soda
1 teaspoon salt
1 1/2 cups semi-sweet chocolate chips
1 1/2 cups butterscotch chips
1 cup coarsely chopped walnuts

Cream the butter and sugars together by hand or with an electric mixer. Add the eggs and vanilla extract. Beat until fluffy. In a separate bowl, combine the flour, baking soda, and salt. Add to the butter mixture and stir or mix well. Stir in the chips and walnuts. Drop golf ball sized portions onto a non-greased cookie sheet. Bake in a preheated 325° oven for 15-20 minutes. They should be golden brown. Use the longer time for a crisper cookie.

Cool on brown paper or racks. Makes 2 dozen cookies.

You can substitute the chips and walnuts with whatever comforts you or your family and friends—other chip varieties—they now have Reeses's and M&M chips, raisins, other kinds of chopped nuts. These are especially comforting when they're still warm and the chips haven't hardened.

Betty's Oatmeal Lace Cookies

1 cup brown sugar
1 cup white sugar
3 sticks unsalted butter
2 large eggs
1 1/2 cups all-purpose flour
1 teaspoon salt
1 teaspoon soda
3 cups quick cooking oatmeal
1/2 cup chopped walnuts
1/2 teaspoon vanilla

Cream the butter and sugar together thoroughly. Beat the eggs and add them and the vanilla to the mixture. Sift the flour, salt, and baking soda together and add to the mixture. Mix well. Add the oatmeal and the nuts. Mold the mixture into three logs, wrap in saran or waxed paper, and refrigerate for 24 hours. These will keep in the refrigerator for two weeks or the dough may be frozen.

To bake, preheat the oven to 375° and slice the log into 1/4" rounds. Place on greased baking sheets, at least 2-3" apart as they spread. Bake for 6-8 minutes until brown, checking after 6 minutes. Remove from the sheets immediately before they start to cool and harden. Faith cuts up brown paper bags for the crispest cookies. Store in a tin or cookie jar.

Makes 9 dozen.

Rhubarb Crumble

1/2 cup walnuts
1 cup flour
1/2 cup rolled oats
1/3 cup packed light brown sugar
1/2 teaspoon cinnamon
Pinch of salt
1/2 cup unsalted butter at room temperature
2 pounds of rhubarb
3/4 to 1 cup white sugar
3 tablespoons flour

Preheat the oven to 375° F. Toast the walnuts in a baking pan until lightly browned and aromatic. Let cool and coarsely chop.
Combine the flour, oats, brown sugar, cinnamon, salt and stir to mix. Working quickly with your hands or a pastry blender, add the butter until the mixture has a crumbly texture. Stir in the chopped walnuts and set aside.

Wash and trim the rhubarb and cut it into 1/2" slices (about 6 cups).

Put the rhubarb in a large bowl and add the sugar and flour. Toss until the rhubarb is well coated. Spread the rhubarb evenly into a 12" baking dish. Sprinkle the topping over the fruit and bake until the rhubarb is tender and bubbling, approximately 45 minutes to an hour. Serve warm with ice cream or whipped cream, if desired.

Faith also makes this with strawberries, both fruits happily in season at the same time. You simply replace half or more of the rhubarb with halved berries.

Norwegian Christmas Cake—Mør Monsen's Kake

>*2 teaspoons unsalted butter, softened*
>*1 pound unsalted butter, softened*
>*2 cups white sugar*
>*4 large eggs*
>*2 cups flour*
>*1 teaspoon vanilla extract*
>*1/2 cup finely chopped blanched almonds*
>*1/4 cup currants*

Preheat the oven to 375°

Using a paper towel, spread a 12x18 inch jelly-roll pan with 2 teaspoons of butter

Cream the remaining butter and the sugar together with an electric mixer. When light and fluffy, beat in the eggs—one at a time—and then the flour and vanilla.

Spread the batter evenly onto the pan and sprinkle with the chopped almonds and currants.

Bake 20-25 minutes, until the surface is a light gold.

Remove from the oven and let the cake cool in the pan.
Cut the cake into diamonds, or squares, with a sharp knife.

This cake may be made up to 2 weeks before Christmas but must then be wrapped in aluminum foil or placed in an airtight tin. Makes about 2 dozen small cakes.

Helen Barer was the high bidder at an auction benefiting the John L. Gildner Regional Institute for Children and Adolescents held at Malice Domestic XX, a convention in the Washington, DC area for mystery lovers. The prize was the opportunity to submit a recipe to Faith's cookbook. When I received Helen's recipe, I was amazed. It's one we make every Christmas—the original recipe came from my Norwegian grandmother.

It turns out that Helen, then Helen Isaacs, was a researcher and writer for the Time-Life Foods of the World series, produced in the mid to late 1960s. I have almost all of these large, beautifully illustrated hardcover cookbooks that came with a handy, smaller spiral bound paperback with the recipes. They sometimes turn up in library or other book sales and are well worth having. Helen was working on the Scandinavian one and "I had a delightful time reading through old cookbooks, talking to Scandinavian cooks, etc." She was "thrilled" to travel throughout Scandinavia on her first overseas assignment and was introduced to this recipe and others.

In the Time-Life book, the chapter in which the recipe appears is titled, "Christmas: Antidote to Darkness"—an extremely apt description of this time of year with many bleak months yet ahead. Christmas Eve is celebrated in Scandinavia rather than Christmas Day and I have wonderful memories of these gatherings with my grandparents, uncles, aunts, and cousins feasting on traditional foods and singing carols in both languages.

There really was a Mother or Mør Monsen. She owned a hotel / restaurant on Norway's West Coast, which is still serving these treats as patrons gaze out at the fjord.

French Apple Cake

2 cups sliced, peeled cooking apples
Juice of 1/2 lemon
1/2 cup sugar
1/4 teaspoon grated nutmeg or cinnamon
1 tablespoon cassis (optional)
1 tablespoon flour
3 tablespoons unsalted melted butter
1 cup sifted all-purpose flour
1/3 cup sugar
1 teaspoon baking powder
1/4 teaspoon salt
1/4 cup milk
1 egg plus 1 egg yolk
1 tablespoon melted butter

Preheat the oven to 400°. Grease a cake pan. Toss the apples with the lemon juice and arrange in a spiral on the bottom of the pan, Cover the pan completely, overlapping the slices if necessary. Sprinkle with the sugar and nutmeg. Dredge with the tablespoon of flour and drizzle with the cassis, if used, then with the melted butter. Set the pan aside while preparing the batter.

Sift the flour, sugar, baking powder, and salt together. Beat the milk, eggs and melted butter together. Add the liquid mixture to the dry ingredients and stir until you have a thick, smooth batter.

Spread the batter on top of the fruit and bake for 25 minutes. Do not overcook. It should be light brown on top. Cool slightly and invert on a serving plate. Serve warm or at room temperature with a small dollop of whipped cream. This cake is also delicious when made with peaches or pears.

Manhattan Morsels

1/2 cup unsalted butter
2 (1 oz.) squares semi-sweet baking chocolate
1 cup sifted all-purpose flour
1/2 teaspoon baking powder
1/2 teaspoon baking soda
1/4 teaspoon salt
2 eggs
1/2 cup white sugar
1/2 cup brown sugar
1 teaspoon vanilla extract
1/2 cup applesauce
1/2 cup chopped walnuts

Preheat the oven to 350°. Grease a 13x9x2 baking pan and set aside. Melt the butter and chocolate in the top of a double boiler. Cool slightly. Sift the flour, baking powder, baking soda, and salt together.

Set aside. Beat the eggs, sugar and vanilla together, then add the chocolate/butter mixture and applesauce, mixing well. Stir in the dry ingredients and mix well again. Add the walnuts, stir and pour into the greased pan.

Bake in the middle of the oven for approximately 25 minutes. Cool in the pan on a rack. This recipe makes 24 squares.

Bainbridge Butterscotch Shortbread

1 cup unsalted butter
1/2 cup dark brown sugar
2 cups flour
1/2 teaspoon baking powder
1/4 teaspoon salt
1 cup finely chopped walnuts or pecans

Sift the flour, salt, and baking powder together and set aside. Cream the butter until soft and gradually add the sugar. Add the flour mixture a little at a time and mix well. Refrigerate for one hour.

Divide the dough in half and keep one portion in the refrigerator while rolling out the other to approximately 1/4" thickness. (The dough gets soft quickly). Sprinkle the dough with the nuts and gently press them in with a rolling pin. Cut into 1 1/2" squares.

Pix uses a paper pattern as she is hopeless at estimating things like this, unlike Faith. Prick with a fork and place the squares on an ungreased cookie sheet. Repeat with the rest of the dough.

Bake until golden brown, approximately 15 minutes in a preheated 350° oven. Makes 6 dozen squares. This is a devastatingly rich, crumbly cookie.

Oatmeal Chocolate Goodies

1/2 cup sugar
2 tablespoons cocoa powder
1/2 cup milk
1/2 cup unsalted butter
1 teaspoon vanilla
1/2 cup peanut butter
3 cups uncooked oatmeal

Bring the milk to a boil and add the sugar, cocoa and butter. Stir until the butter melts. Turn the heat down and cook for 1 1/2 minutes, stirring constantly. Remove from the heat and add the vanilla and peanut butter. Stir and add the oatmeal. Mix well. Drop teaspoons of the mixture onto a cookie sheet covered with waxed paper. Refrigerate until firm. Makes 4 dozen cookies. Store in a tin, the layers separated by wax paper, in the refrigerator or a cool place.

Small children, and other free spirits, enjoy mixing the oatmeal and dropping the mixture onto the waxed paper with their hands.

Faith Fairchild's Maine Blueberry Tarte

Pastry:

1 1/2 cups flour
1 tablespoon sugar
A pinch of salt
1 or 2 Tablespoons unsalted butter
3 tablespoons ice water

Filling:

3 cups blueberries
4 tablespoons sugar
2 tablespoons flour
1 tablespoon lemon juice

Put the flour, sugar, and salt in the bowl of a food processor. Pulse once. Cut the butter into pieces and add to the dry ingredients. Pulse again until the mixture resembles coarsely ground cornmeal. (You may also cut the butter into the flour mixture with two knives or a pastry cutter.)

Add the ice water through the feeder tube with the motor running and briefly process until a ball is formed. Wrap the dough in waxed paper or plastic wrap and refrigerate for 1/2 hour. Faith makes ice water by adding a few cubes to a glass of water before she starts to make the dough.

Roll out the dough on a lightly floured surface and line a 10" fluted tarte pan—the kind with the bottom that comes out. Prick the bottom of the dough-lined pan with a fork.

Combine 2 tablespoons of flour with 2 tablespoons of sugar and dust the bottom.

Add the lemon juice to the fruit and spread evenly over the dough. Sprinkle 2 tablespoons of sugar on top and place on a baking sheet. Bake in the middle of a preheated 375° oven for 40 minutes, or until the edges turn slightly brown. Let cool for 10 minutes and remove from the pan to a serving plate.

Tastes best warm or at room temperature. Serves 10. This recipe is also delicious with other summer fruits. Caution: do not use frozen blueberries or you will have a soggy mess. Pix knows.

Pelham Fudge Cake

3 squares unsweetened chocolate
1/2 cup water
2 cups sifted cake flour
1 1/2 teaspoon baking powder
1 teaspoon baking soda
1 teaspoon salt
1 cup sour cream
2/3 cup unsalted butter
2/3 cup firmly packed dark brown sugar
1 cup white sugar
3 large eggs
2 teaspoons vanilla

Melt the chocolate in the water over low heat, mix well. Let cool. Sift the flour, baking powder, baking soda, and salt together and set aside. Preheat the oven to 350° F.

Add the sour cream to the thoroughly cooled chocolate.

Cream the butter and sugars together and then add the eggs one at a time, beating after each one. Beat the vanilla into the butter, sugar, egg mixture. Now add the flour mixture and chocolate mixture alternately.

Divide the batter between two round cake pans greased with butter or sprayed with a product like PAM.

Bake in the center of the oven for 35-40 minutes, until a broom straw or cake tester comes out clean.

Fill and frost when cool using your favorite chocolate frosting recipe, adding 3/4 cup chopped walnuts. Faith likes to use a traditional chocolate butter cream frosting and saves some of the walnuts to sprinkle on top of the layer cake.

Lizzie's Sour Cream Brownies

1/2 cup unsalted butter
1 ounce (1 square) unsweetened chocolate
1 ounce (1 square) semi-sweet chocolate
2 eggs
1 cup sugar
1 teaspoon vanilla
1/2 cup flour, sifted
Pinch of salt
1/4 cup sour cream
2/3 cup chopped walnuts (optional)

Preheat the oven to 350°. Grease and lightly flour an 8-inch square pan. Melt the butter and chocolate in the top of a double boil. Cool to room temperature. Beat the eggs and sugar together until they form a lemony ribbon. Add the vanilla. Fold the chocolate and butter into the egg mixture. Then fold in the flour, salt, and sour cream. Add the nuts if used.

Bake for 30 minutes in the middle of the oven. Do not overcook.

Let cool 30 minutes before cutting. Cooking at 325° will give you very moist brownie, which Faith likes to do sometimes.

This is a very rich, dense brownie, similar in texture to flourless chocolate cake. It's sinfully good with ice cream on top. Makes 16 good-sized brownies. If you double the recipe, you have to do it in two batches.

Pepperkaker (Ginger Snaps)

2/3 cup butter (1 stick plus 2 2/3 tablespoons)
1/3 cup brown sugar
1/3 cup white sugar
1 tablespoon molasses
1 1/2 teaspoons ground cloves
2 1/4 teaspoons cinnamon
2 1/4 teaspoons ginger
1 teaspoon baking soda
1/4 cup boiling water
2 1/2 cups flour

Heat the butter, sugars, and molasses in a heavy saucepan over low heat until the butter melts. Remove the pan from the heat and stir in the spices. Transfer the mixture to a bowl and let cool for 5 minutes. Mix the soda with the boiling water and add to the bowl. Stir in the flour, mixing well to make a smooth dough. Refrigerate for at least an hour.

Preheat the oven to 325°.

Working in batches, roll the dough to approximately 1/2" thick. These cookies are best when thin and crisp. This recipe used a heart and fluted round cutter, each 2" across. Bake the cookies on lightly buttered sheets for 8-10 minutes. Transfer immediately to cool on brown paper or racks. Makes approximately 6 dozen cookies. Store the cookies in an airtight tin. The dough may also be frozen.

Pepperkaker are made all year long, but are essential at Christmas. Families with small children have a pepperkaker baking day just before the holiday. The dough is cut into many shapes: hearts, stars, men, women, pigs and other farm animals. White icing is piped onto the cooled cookies to decorate them. My cousin, Hege, relates that the dough is so good that at these parties usually only half makes it into the oven!

Mrs. Mallory's Peanut Butter Cookies

1 1/3 cups flour
1/2 teaspoon baking powder
1/3 teaspoon baking soda
1 stick unsalted butter
1/2 cup chunky or plain peanut butter
3/4 cup firmly packed brown sugar
1/4 cup white sugar
1 teaspoon vanilla extract
Chocolate kisses

Preheat the oven to 350°. Sift the flour, baking powder and soda together and set aside. Cream the butter, peanut butter and sugars together. Add the egg and vanilla. Beat well, add the flour mixture and beat again. Shape into balls and place on an ungreased cookie sheet, leaving 2" between the cookies.

Cook for 8 minutes, push the chocolate kisses in, and cook for 2 more minutes. Cool on racks. (Although this taste sinfully delicious warm). Makes 4 dozen.

You may also use Hugs, small chocolate kisses covered with white chocolate.

Lizzie's Flourless Peanut Butter Cookies

1 cup chunky or plain peanut butter
1 cup sugar
1 large egg
1 teaspoon baking soda
1/2 teaspoon vanilla extract
1 cup miniature chocolate chips

Preheat oven to 350°. Mix the first five ingredients in a bowl and add the chocolate chips. Mix well. Using moistened hands (the dough is sticky), form 1 tablespoon of the dough into balls. Place about 2 inches apart on an ungreased cookie sheet.

Bake for approximately 12 minutes until the cookies are puffy, but still soft to the touch. Immediately transfer to racks to cool.

This is one of those Godsend bake sale or need dessert quickly recipes and Faith made sure to teach it to her students.

Lizzie's Sugar and Spice Cookies

3/4 cup unsalted butter
1 cup sugar
1 egg, slightly beaten
1/4 cup molasses
2 cups flour
2 teaspoons baking soda
1 teaspoon cinnamon
3/4 teaspoon ground cloves
3/4 teaspoon ground ginger
1/4 teaspoon salt
Sugar

Preheat the oven to 375°.

Cream the butter, sugar, egg, and molasses together thoroughly.

Sift the flour, baking soda, spices, and salt together.

Add to the butter mixture and stir.

Roll the dough into balls, 1 inch in diameter, and roll the balls in sugar. Set approximately 2 inches apart on a lightly greased cookie sheet and bake for 12 minutes. Let cool on brown paper or racks.

Makes approximately 4 dozen cookies. For an elegant tea cookie, make 1/2 inch diameter balls and reduce the cooking time to 9 minutes. makes approximately 8 dozen.

Denouement Apple / Pear Crisp

1 3/4-2 pounds apples or pears
Juice of one 1/2 lemon
2 tablespoons maple syrup
3/4 cup flour
1/4 teaspoon salt
3 tablespoons brown sugar
6 tablespoons unsalted butter

Preheat the oven to 375°.

Peel, core, and slice the fruit. Toss in a bowl with the lemon juice to prevent browning.

Place the slices in a lightly buttered baking dish. Drizzle with the maple syrup.

Put the flour, salt, sugar, and butter in the bowl of a food processor fitted with a metal blade and process Briefly. Or you may cut the butter in with a pastry cutter or two knives. The mixture should be crumbly.

Cover the fruit evenly with the flour mixture and bake for 45 minutes or until the juices are bubbling.

Let sit for 5 minutes and serve with whipped cream, vanilla ice cream, or crème fraîche.

This recipe may be made with pears or apples. It is especially delicious with a mixture of apples, such as Empire and Delicious (sweet) or Macoun and Macintosh (slightly tart).

(Virtually) Flourless Chocolates Cakes

8 ounces bittersweet chocolate, broken into small pieces
1 stick unsalted butter plus a small amount to grease ramekins
3 large eggs
2 egg yolks
1/3 cup sugar
2 tablespoons flour plus a small amount to dust ramekins
Confectioner's sugar

Preheat the oven to 425°. Butter and lightly dust six 4 ounce ovenproof ramekins with flour. Gently heat the chocolate and butter in the top of a double boiler, stirring often. For a sweeter cake, use sweeter chocolate. Using a whisk or electric mixer, beat the eggs, yolks and sugar together until thickened and foamy.

Beat the melted butter/chocolate mixture into the egg/sugar mixture and immediately add the flour, beating well to avoid air holes. Pour the batter into the ramekins. The dessert may be covered with plastic wrap and refrigerated at this point. Bring it to room temperature before cooking. Place the ramekins on a tray and bake in the middle of the oven for 10 minutes. The centers of the cakes should be very soft.

Unmold on dessert plates and sift some confectioner's sugar on top.

Serve immediately!

Chocolate Crunch Cookies

1/2 lb. unsalted butter
1 cup brown sugar
1 egg yolk
2 cups sifted flour
1 tsp. vanilla extract
1 1/2 cups dark or semi-sweet chocolate bits combined with 1/2 cup toffee bits
1/2 cup toffee bits for topping

Cream the butter and sugar. Add the egg yolk and beat until smooth. Add the flour, mix, then add the vanilla. At this stage, Faith uses her hands as the dough tends to be crumbly. Knead until smooth.

Spread the dough in a greased 9x12 baking pan and place in the middle of a preheated 350° oven. Again Faith finds that it is easier to pat the dough evenly into the pan using her hands.

Bake for twenty-five minutes and take the pan out of the oven.

Distribute the chocolate/toffee bit mixture evenly over the cookie layer and bake for four minutes more.

Remove the pan from the oven and immediately spread the melted chocolate / toffee mixture. Sprinkle what is now the frosting with the remaining toffee bits.

It is important to let the cookies cool completely in the pan before cutting into squares.

This is a decadently rich cookie and makes either twenty-four or thirty-six cookies. It's up to you.

The Body in the Sleigh

The Body in the Sleigh is dedicated to librarians and I want to write about them and libraries, but first a bit about how this book came to be written. In 2003 I wrote a short story, "The Two Marys," which was published in the 2004 Avon collection, *Mistletoe and Mayhem*. Over the years I've heard authors talk about falling in love with their characters and said characters taking over. I had never had those experiences, although I'm extremely fond of Faith Fairchild and it would be wonderful if she could take over, saving me from the task of writing about her—some sort of automatic writing, perhaps? I'd have more time to read, for one thing. And then I did fall in love—with Mary Bethany and Miriam Carpenter. And, in a way, they took over.

By definition, a short story is short, but as I wrote it I kept wanting to write more about these two women, much more. I wanted to write about their childhoods and I wanted to write about the two of them together. I wanted to write Faith into more scenes. I was happy with the way the story came out and was honored when Malice Domestic nominated it for an Agatha Award, but I kept wishing I had been able to write a novel instead. When I mentioned it to my agent, Faith Hamlin—(serendipitous note: I wrote the first book prior to meeting this Faith)—she said, "Why not?" Why not indeed and I was off, free to write about these two women, and all sorts of new characters, to my heart's content. What resulted was not simply an expansion of the short story, as I planned originally, but a completely new tale and one that has become very dear to me. This is because of the message of the season and the people whose paths crossed at that time of the year. I admit to getting choked up when I wrote about Jake and Norah and read the last lines in the Epilogue.

And now to libraries.

Henry Ward Beecher, brother to Harriet, wrote: "A library is not a luxury but one of the necessities of life." My first library was housed in an old farmhouse in Livingston, New Jersey. Today, the town I grew up in bears little resemblance to the small, farming community it was in the early 1950's when we moved there. The children's room in the Livingston Public Library had been the kitchen and although it wasn't in use, the old cook stove was still there. Removing it would have been quite a project. Bookshelves lined the walls and there was a window seat where I would curl up to read while I waited for the rest of the family to select their books. Out the window I could see a few apple trees, remnants of the orchard, and beyond them, across the street, the first of what would be many new stores and offices. I worked my way around the kitchen walls reading about the March family, the Moffats, *All-of-a-Kind Family*, *Ballet Shoes* and the other shoes, *Misty of Chincoteague* and the other horses, and all the Landmark books.

Mrs. Ruth Rockwood was the librarian, custodian not only of the town's library, but also of much of its history. With my parents and others, she started the Livingston Historical Society. When I was about nine, I had exhausted the kitchen's offerings and she allowed me to enter the parlor and dining room—the adult section! Books did not line the walls here, but were arranged in floor to ceiling stacks. The wood floors were brightly polished, although the room that had been created was a little dark—the windows had been partially obscured by all the books. I thought it was the most wonderful place in the world. Each week Mrs. Rockwood would pick out a book for me to take home and read. The first was *A Lantern in Her Hand*, a tale about a Nebraska pioneer woman written in 1928 by Bess Streeter Aldrich. I loved it and after reading that canon progressed to Frances Parkinson Keyes (including *Dinner at Antoine's*, her only mystery), and Marjorie Kinnan Rawlings—Mrs. Rockwood's favorite authors, I assume. My home was filled with books and Ruth Rockwood didn't instill my love of reading, but fanned the flames. What she did instill was a lifelong passion for libraries and librarians.

Eventually the town built a fancy brick library that matched the other new municipal buildings. I was in high school by then and had transferred some of my loyalty to the LHS library and librarian, Mrs. Galford. I was a library aide with my friend, Ellen McNaught. We never minded shelving books, since we got to see what had just been returned, discovering Conrad Richter—*The Trees*, such a great book—and Mary Stewart's *Madame, Will You Talk?*, which took us to the others of this vastly underrated writer. Even now, I gravitate to the "To Be Shelved" or "Recent Returns" in my town library. It's like a smorgasbord.

I'm sure Ellen and I felt very important stamping cards with the wooden-handled date device that had to be checked each morning to make sure it was accurate. I also recall we were not above leafing through *The Dictionary of American Slang*, which was kept behind the desk, not because Mrs. Galford believed in withholding information, but because a certain group of boys was destroying the binding and causing it to flop open at several juicy entries.

Touring Wellesley College before applying, the beautiful lakeside setting was a plus; Professor David Ferry's poetry class and his recitation of Yeats's "Lake Isle of Innisfree" an inspiration (I was ready to "arise and go" right then and there wherever Professor Ferry might lead); but it was the library that sold me. The Rare Books Room actually has the door to 50 Wimpole Street with the brass letter slot through which Robert Browning slipped missives to Elizabeth Barrett! During exam times we used to try to get locked in the library overnight at exam times by hiding in the lavatories. The "libe" closed at an hour presumably intended to give us a decent night's sleep. The custodian always discovered us, but before he did there was a delicious sense of being almost alone with all those marvelous books.

I somehow find myself in my local library several times a week. Often it's to consult Jeanne Bracken, reference librarian extraordinaire, or I'm lured in by the thought of new books, new titles, although I have stacks of my own to read or re-read at home.

Librarians are my favorite people and libraries my favorite places to be. I'm a member of six Friends of the Library groups. I enjoy giving talks at libraries, especially at meetings of the American Library Association, the Public Library Association, the Massachusetts Library Association—what's the collective for "librarians," as in a pride of lions, "a tome?" "a volume?"—library book festivals or fundraisers where patrons whoop it up all for the sake of words. Having just returned from Hagerstown, Maryland and their "Gala in the Stacks: Let's Jazz It Up" benefiting the Washington County Free Library Capital campaign, I really do mean "whoop." Speaking to the revelers, I mentioned the fact that the access to libraries, and therefore information, that we enjoy in this country is rare worldwide. I can use my Minuteman Library Network card at over 40 local libraries. Simply walk in, check out a book or some other material, use their computers with no questions asked, no fee required, and nothing under lock and key. In addition to their roles as providers, librarians are also protectors.

They're a feisty bunch. I've always thought so, even before the librarian action figure came out. It's modeled on Nancy Pearl, the Seattle librarian author of *Book Lust* and *More Book Lust*. The figure's hand comes up to her lips to shush patrons, a gesture I have never seen a real librarian use. More accurate would have been a librarian waving an arm in protest. In my mind's eye, I envision librarians atop barricades, protecting our civil liberties, guarding our rights to privacy, and unbanning books.

Ultimately librarians are matchmakers. They introduce us to new authors and subjects. They connect us with needed information and, if we like, will teach us how to find it ourselves. They embrace new technology and draw us in, as well. Traveling to libraries all across the country, I have been reminded how they also function as gathering places. New libraries have small auditoria that are available to community groups for meetings and events. Comfortable places to sit and read, yes, but many libraries are adding cafes where patrons can meet for coffee. I loved my little Livingston farmhouse library and the small, gray shingled Chase Emerson Library in Deer Isle, Maine, but I admit to detours whenever I'm in town to see the McKim courtyard and Sargent murals at the Boston Public Library—the oldest municipal public library in the country and the largest—and the Rose Reading Room at The New York Public Library, pausing outside on Fifth Avenue to pat one of the stone lions, "Patience" and "Fortitude." Our jewel is the crown is, of course, The Library of Congress—again unique in the access it provides and its preservation of books and documents. (There is still a card catalogue as a backup to the Virtual one). The Great Hall is splendid. Participating in a panel at the library was an honor and memory I will always hold dear.

Libraries have functioned as centers of learning since Alexandria, but now more than ever in these economic times, they are providing instruction that individuals cannot afford to take elsewhere. Courses in ESL, literacy, computer literacy, taxes, writing of all sorts, and book groups for every taste are standard fare. Andrew Carnegie suggested "Let There Be Light" with the rays of a rising sun be set in the stone above the entrances to his free libraries. It's as apt now as it was in the 19th century. Yes, librarians are keepers of the light as well as matchmakers—and it's a match made in heaven. The dedication of this book is long overdue.

APPENDIX: LIST OF RECIPES BY BOOK

The Body in the Cast
Unadulterated Black Bean
 Soup
Norwegian Meatballs
Pear Brie Pizzette
Denoument Apple/Pear Crisp
Lizzie's Sugar and Spice
 Cookies

The Body in the Basement
Pix Rowe Miller's Family Fish
 Chowder
Louise Frazier's Southern Corn
Bread
Faith's Emergency Sewing
Circle Spreads:
Chutney Cheese and Chèvre
 with Herbs
Bainbridge Butterscotch
Shortbread
Faith Fairchild's Maine
Blueberry Tarte

The Body in the Bog
Cardamon Raisin Bread
Patriots' Day Pancakes
Chocolate Crunch Cookies
Faith's Yankee Pot Roast
Aleford Bakes Beans

The Body in the Fjord
Fiskepudding with Shrimp
 Sauce
Cucumber and Dill Salad
Lutefisk
Smørbrød Open-Faced
 Sandwiches
Vafler Sour Cream Waffles
Pepperkaker Ginger Snaps

The Body in the Bookcase
Avocado Bisque
Chicken Liver and Mushroom
 Pâté
Polenta with Gorgonzola
Mini Zucchini Fritters
Oatmeal Chocolate Goodies
Lizzie's Sour Cream Brownies

The Body in the Big Apple
Pork Loin Stuffed with Winter
 Fruits
Waldorf Salad
Big Apple Pancakes
French Apple Cake
Manhattan Morsels

The Body in the Moonlight
Chèvre, Roasted Pepper,
  and Red Onion Sandwich
Coq Au Vin
Salad with Warm Cheese
Toasts
Doughnut Muffins
Betty's Oatmeal Lace Cookies

The Body in the Bonfire
Pasta E Fagioli With Sausage
Smothered Pork Chops
Pasta Frittata
Mrs. Mallory's Peanut Butter
  Cookies
Lizzie's Flourless Peanut Butter
Cookies
Flourless Chocolate Cake

The Body in the Lighthouse
Corn Pudding
Crab Cakes
Blueberry Muffins
Pasta With Smoked Chicken
  and Summer Vegetables
Comfort Cookies

The Body in the Attic
Butternut Squash Soup
Alsatian Onion Tarte
Cousin Luise's Linguini
  With Asparagas
Cambridge Tea Cake
Harvard Squares

The Body in the Snowdrift
Apology Mushroom Soup
Llapingachos with Salsa
  De Mali (Potato Cakes
  With Peanut Sauce)
Spanakopita
Glad's Brownies
Aunt Susie's Cake

The Body in The Ivy
Asian Noodles With Crabmeat
Boeuf Bourguinon
Fennel Soup
Rhubarb Crumble
Pelham Fudge cake

The Body in the Gallery
Chicken Stroganoff
Endive Spears with Chèvre
Pantry Fridge Soup
Parsnip Puree
Red Velvet Cake

The Body in the Sleigh
Seafood Risotto
The Annie Breakfast Sandwich
Pumpkin Pie Soup
Chocolate Bread Pudding
Mother Monsen's Cake